Strategic Planning for Local Government

Strategic Planning for
Local Government

The International City/County Management Association is the professional and educational organization for chief appointed management executives in local government. The purposes of ICMA are to enhance the quality of local government and to nurture and assist professional local government administrators in the United States and other countries. In furtherance of its mission, ICMA develops and disseminates new approaches to management through training programs, information services, and publications.

Managers, carrying a wide range of titles, serve cities, towns, counties, councils of governments, and state/provincial associations of local governments throughout the world. These managers serve at the direction of elected councils and governing boards. ICMA serves these managers and local governments through many programs that aim at improving the manager's professional competence and strengthening the quality of all local governments.

The International City/County Management Association was founded in 1914; adopted its City Management Code of Ethics in 1924; and established its Institute for Training in Municipal Administration in 1934. The Institute, in turn, provided the basis for the Municipal Management Series, generally termed the "ICMA Green Books."

ICMA's interests and activities include public management education; standards of ethics for members; the *Municipal Year Book* and other data services; urban research; and newsletters, the monthly magazine *Public Management,* and other publications. ICMA's efforts for the improvement of local government management—as represented by this book—are offered for all local governments and educational institutions.

Strategic Planning for Local Government

Gerald L. Gordon

PRACTICAL MANAGEMENT SERIES
Barbara H. Moore, Editor

Strategic Planning for Local Government
Balanced Growth
Capital Financing Strategies for Local Governments
Capital Projects
Current Issues in Leisure Services
The Entrepreneur in Local Government
Ethical Insight, Ethical Action
Hazardous Materials, Hazardous Waste
Human Services on a Limited Budget
Local Economic Development
Long-Term Financial Planning
Managing for Tomorrow
Managing New Technologies
Pay and Benefits
Performance Evaluation
Personnel Practices for the '90s
Police Practice in the '90s
Practical Financial Management
Productivity Improvement Techniques
Shaping the Local Economy
Successful Negotiating in Local Government
Telecommunications for Local Government

Library of Congress Cataloging-in-Publication Data

Gordon, Gerald L.
    Strategic planning for local government / Gerald L. Gordon.
        p.   cm. — (Practical management series)
    Includes bibliographic references.
    ISBN 0-87326-065-1
    1. Political planning—United States. 2. Strategic planning—
United States. 3. Local government—United States. I. Title.
II. Series.
JS344.F4G67   1993
352'.000472'0973—dc20   93-401
                                                          CIP

Printed in the United States of America.
989796959493
54321

Foreword

In a tight and rapidly changing economy, many local governments are cutting back, "right-sizing," and changing the way they do business. At the same time, managers know that the year 2000 is just around the corner, and it's their responsibility to position the community for the next century at the same time they grapple with the problems of today.

In this environment, strategic planning is becoming increasingly popular as a tool for examining and planning for likely future scenarios. It allows a community to manage for the future instead of reacting to events as they occur.

This book was written for local governments and those who work with them. It provides step-by-step guidance for the development of sound strategic plans that can help our communities establish and achieve future goals and objectives. As part of ICMA's Practical Management Series, it is devoted to serving local officials' needs for timely information on current issues and problems.

ICMA is grateful to Gerald L. Gordon for his diligent efforts in developing the book, to Sandy Chizinsky Leas for her initial editorial contributions, and to the individuals and organizations who developed the plans that are reprinted in part in this volume.

William H. Hansell, Jr.
Executive Director
ICMA

About the Author

Gerald L. Gordon is Executive Director of the Fairfax County (Virginia) Economic Development Authority. Previously, he was Director of Employment and Training Programs, Arlington County, Virginia; Planner, Fairfax County Manpower Administration; and Manpower Development Specialist, U.S. Department of Labor. He has taught planning, forecasting, and other management topics at several colleges and universities. Dr. Gordon has a B.A. degree from The Citadel, an M.A. degree from George Washington University, and a Ph.D. degree from the Catholic University of America.

Contents

CHAPTER 6
The Role of Forecasting

CHAPTER 7
Summary and Conclusions

CHAPTER 8
Strategic Planning: A Step-by-Step Guide

APPENDIXES

Introduction

Strategic planning is a process by which an organization attempts to control its destiny rather than allowing future events to do so. By appraising future opportunities and its own existing and future strengths and weaknesses, an organization can help ensure its success and avoid identifiable problems. Following the lead of the business community, local governments have come to embrace the concept of strategic planning over the past decade.

As distant countries and their markets have grown closer through technological advances, and as the face of competition has changed, new opportunities have been created. And new opportunities carry attendant risks. In the private sector, if companies are going to minimize the risks inherent in their attempts to maximize profits, they must establish formal planning systems to replace older, informal, intuitive methods. The business world has generally accepted this premise, and local governments have followed suit, adapting strategic planning methods to their own needs.

As acceptance of strategic planning has grown, so has the body of literature which examines its various aspects and applications. These books and journals have proven useful. Business executives have learned the value of scrutinizing shifts in existing markets, the evolution of new markets, changes in the domestic economy and in foreign markets, and other environmental factors that affect the ability of a corporation to achieve its goals and objectives.

The lion's share of research and scholarly thought has been devoted to the impact of planning on profit, market share, and return on investment. Yet the same environmental factors that affect a business's bottom line can also affect an organization's ability to be successful. It is this realization that has spurred local governments to undertake strategic planning.

This book addresses strategic planning in the context of local governments, whose primary orientation is not the "bottom line," but the provision of service to the public with finite resources and motives other than profit.

Despite this fundamental difference from a business, a local government must have the same orientation to the present and the future as a company. A business has short-term profit and market-share targets; a local government has short-term service provision goals. A business must plan for future growth in existing and new markets; a local government must plan for future demands for public services with either a shrinking, a static, or an expanding pool of human and capital resources. In short, a local government must satisfy today's needs for constituent services and seek means of providing improved services in the years to come.

This is not to say that strategic planning is easy to implement. Taking a long term view may run counter to a government's existing practice of one- to two-year planning. To some extent, this choice is and must be driven by budgetary considerations. The ability of a local government to provide public services depends on the availability of revenues and other resources necessary to support them. Tax revenues are difficult to project far into the future, and federal and state allocations to cities and counties are constantly fluctuating. Planning helps a community to identify and mobilize its available resources and to use them for the most pressing community needs. Planning can have tremendous value in bolstering citizens' confidence in the future. It will aid in the assessment of current practices, validate or refute currently held assumptions, facilitate networking between various groups in the community, and increase everyone's knowledge of and appreciation for local elected officials, professional staff, and citizen volunteers.

Many communities have already recognized the value of strategic planning in the same way that many companies have. One small town which initiated an ambitious planning process indicated it needed the process to:

- provide a plausible interpretation of the future and a sense of direction and enthusiasm
- foster cooperation and consistency between actions taken by public, private, and educational sectors
- prioritize initiatives which have wide community support
- make better use of community support
- ensure government is appropriately organized to respond to priorities.

As noted earlier, most of the literature on strategic planning focuses on the private sector; yet many of the lessons are applicable to public-sector strategic planning as well.

It is the intent of this book to draw these lessons from the private sector planning literature and to introduce some practical applications for public sector bodies in a format which can be used by public officials as they work to anticipate the future and to develop strategies for maximizing opportunities and minimizing threats.

Like business, local government must be responsive to change in its environment. A business does so to determine how best to allocate personnel, equipment, and capital to maximize return on investment. A local government must also allocate human and capital resources to the best advantage, but the stakes are different.

For a local government, decisions affect more than new markets or profit margins. They affect people's lives: the basic human needs for safety, food, clothing, and shelter; and the secondary needs for education, a physical infrastructure, and more.

In order to provide more, or more effective services, local government needs to assess what the demands will be and the relative value of competing needs. All of this must be accomplished against an almost certain assumption: the sum of all valid needs will exceed the availability of resources. To compound this dilemma of political reality, the allocation of scarce resources is based on an imperfect understanding of future needs.

As the economy becomes more complex, the nature and the rapidity of change become more important in determining future constituent needs and in constraining the ability of local government to meet them. As an area's demographic makeup changes, services must adapt. As the rate of technological change increases, organizations must respond more diligently. As regulations come and go, entities must react. As the environment in which an organization must operate becomes more complex, its leadership must become more sensitive to those complexities and to the degree and types of change needed. In short, leaders must have a realistic vision of the future and strategies to pursue that vision.

But cities, towns, and counties have only recently begun to plan their futures in a conscious and systematic way. The absence of planning and its benefits is frequently noted by cities which are initiating a strategic planning process. Witness, for example, the following statement from the strategic plan for the city of Cocoa, Florida: "The City has managed its affairs for many years without a documented system linking day-to-day activities to a comprehensive long-term strategy. This document should provide the essential element for a more effective means of determining priorities, allocating limited resources, and measuring progress."

The benefits of strategic planning

To fully appreciate the benefits of strategic planning, it is useful to recognize its nature: it is both a *process* and a *product*. The *process* involves a systematic examination of the organization and its environment by those who have a stake in its future success. The *product* is a document specifying the actions required to achieve future goals based on the information unearthed during the planning process. Together, these components of strategic planning yield numerous benefits to any organization.

Anticipation of the future   First, strategic planning improves the odds that an organization will succeed in its mission by helping its leaders comprehend the future and position the organization within it rather than reacting to future events as they occur. Strategic planning is the anticipation of future problems and opportunities. If these

---

Strategic policy and city management

Mission Statement: Formulate city policies, organizational goals, and administrative objectives, not only to provide an array of services but also innovative methods of financing so as to best serve community needs in the most ethical, equitable, efficient, effective, and democratic means possible.

Strategic Directions: Design organizational strategy on the basis of continuous matching of anticipated opportunities and problems in the external environment with distinctive administrative strengths and limitations in the internal environment.

- Actively participate with City Council in shaping policy, then make sure that the intent of strategy is interpreted into the work of the various departments of the organization. Make the organization more streamlined, flexible and competitive.
- Appraise and refine the existing organization in terms of where tasks critical to the success of the strategy can be performed most effectively. Make clear who does what. Develop key personnel who can push forward in the direction singled out in the strategy.
- Guide the execution of the strategy and policy through the organization by programming, activating, and controlling the operations.
- Provide leadership in specific programming of non-repetitive work, communicating and motivating, and exercising control over the rate and quality of performance.
- Foster the cooperation of employees who convert organizational resources into local government services by relating personnel selection, development, compensation, benefits and labor relations to the successful execution of the selected strategy. This includes the development of a top management team not only to attain strategic objectives through self-management

are identified before they are encountered, they can be either minimized or maximized as appropriate. If they are not identified, opportunities can be missed and problems can grow to insurmountable proportions.

Assessment of the organization   Second, strategic planning forces people within an organization to come together to discuss the strengths and weaknesses of their organization, where they would like to go, and how best to get there.

Community goal setting and consensus building   Third, strategic planning promotes goal-setting and reaching a consensus around

and independent work, but also to involve all employees in a team approach leading to commitment towards excellence and loyalty.

- Utilize integrated data processing as an important aid for organizational control including a management information system that converts financial budget figures into standards that can be compared with actual departmental and organizational performance. Develop optimum use of telecommunications and information management.
- Continue to implement a continuous planning process not only to integrate and balance internal and external forces of change but also to move the organization from its present situation toward future strategic goals.
- Integrate strategy with action-oriented research to improve delivery of socially responsible services.
- Adapt organizational action to new technology, social shifts, political realignments and pressures, and economic changes by identifying crucial aspects of the dynamic environment, making frequent forecasts for each of these aspects, and insuring that such forecasts are actually used by organizational executives in formulating operational plans.
- Identify, examine, and develop quality designs of all the components that create the physical environment of the local community and formulate economic revitalization strategies that encourage public and private investments in such design improvements.
- Develop motivational programs to satisfy employee needs and to provide opportunities for employees to realize their maximum potential while, at the same time, attaining organizational objectives.

Source: Strategic plan, Berkley, Michigan, 1988.

those goals. This enhances the likelihood of achieving the goals. As will be discussed later, establishing goals for an organization requires the give-and-take of negotiation as participants seek ways to align organizational strengths with future opportunities and challenges.

This process tends to result in compromising on commonly accepted targets and programs. This process is more critical in a local government than in a business due to the range and nature of functions for which the government is responsible. Because local government has such a direct influence on people's lives, the process of making decisions about its future often brings disparate views and philosophical disagreements into the open. Thus, the strategic planning process in the public sector must frequently arrive at compromises after painful concessions or even outright disapproval. The process of arriving at such compromises on generally accepted goals should be viewed, however, as a strength of the process as well as a necessary step.

Allocation of resources   Fourth, strategic planning facilitates the ever-difficult process of human and capital resource allocation. All organizations have finite resources to allocate among their products, services, and functions. The allocation of scarce resources must consider all potential demands and the impact of providing one project, service, or function over another. In the corporate sector, these competing demands may be research and development, marketing, and capital investment in new plants. In the public sector, the competing demands are all the services the government provides and the physical infrastructure it maintains.

Establishment of benchmarks   Finally, strategic planning provides benchmarks. The goals and objectives define direction from the beginning of a program or other fiscal or planning cycle. Subsequently, they provide the measurements against which performance can be gauged. Without goals and objectives, an organization cannot know whether it has been successful. Yet, as pointed out by the renowned strategist, Michael Kami, "Very few organizations can actually show you a concise strategic action plan."[1] Organizations would be well advised to heed the advice of the Mad Hatter, who explained to Alice in *Through the Looking Glass*, if you don't know "where you want to get to . . . it doesn't matter which way you go."

Cities, towns, and counties that use strategic planning do so from a clear recognition of the needs for planning summarized above. So evident are these needs, in fact, that the plans often explicitly state the benefits expected to be derived. Such a statement was made in the strategic plan of the city of Berkley, Michigan, as shown in the sidebar on pages 4 and 5.

Preview of the book

This book outlines the strategic planning process for local government officials and those who work with them to anticipate and shape the future of their communities.

Localities conduct strategic planning exercises for different reasons. The impetus may be the need to stop the drain of business, youth, or the general population from an area; or it may be to manage growth. Planning may be driven by one key person to secure the benefits of a future opportunity, or it may be a practice commonly accepted as necessary for the proper management of change. In some localities, the process is a new one, while in other communities plans are in their second or third generation.

Whatever prompts those associated with local governments to engage in strategic planning, and at whatever evolutionary step the process is conducted, the process of planning and the structure of the plan itself will be very similar. This book will assist those involved in strategic planning.

The initial chapters of this book define the terms and describe the process. Subsequent chapters cite examples, real and fictitious, to demonstrate the principles involved. The final chapter provides a step-by-step strategic planning guide for local governments, and extensive appendixes provide examples of written plans from a number of communities. A bibliography of related references is provided at the end of the book.

Excerpts from the strategic plans of ten communities are used throughout this book to provide examples of alternative approaches and presentations: Arlington, Texas; Berkley, Michigan; Catawba County, North Carolina; Clifton, New Jersey; Cocoa, Florida; Outagamie County, Wisconsin; Placentia, California; Santa Clarita, California; Whitley County, Indiana; and Wichita, Kansas.

1.   Michael Kami, *Kami Strategic
     Assumptions* (Lighthouse
     Point, FL: Kami, 1988), p.2.

Chapter 1

What Is Strategic Planning?

Strategic planning in local government is a systematic process by which a community anticipates and plans for its future. The result is a written document that guides the the community toward its future goals. This chapter opens with an overview of the strategic planning process, then takes a look at what strategic planning *is*—what a community can reasonably expect from the process—and what it is *not*.

Overview of strategic planning

The initial recommendation to undertake strategic planning in local government may come from the governing body, from the appointed administrator or administrative staff, or from interest groups within the community. It may be stimulated by a negative event—loss of a major employer or concern over the quality of life in the community. Or it may have a positive motivation—a determination on the part of citizens and local officials to harness the community's strengths and take charge of its future.

Whatever the underlying reason, strategic planning needs to be embraced by the elected leadership and publicized and "sold" to the community and to local government employees. This early stage involves action by the elected council, communication with government employees, face-to-face discussions with future participants in the process, and dissemination of information to the public. As it becomes clear that a decision to undertake strategic planning is imminent, the local government staff must prepare to administer it. One individual should be responsible for formalizing the planning process, identifying and inviting participants, scheduling meetings and establishing deadlines, and ensuring that necessary follow-up steps are taken. This person may be from the manager's office, the planning department, or elsewhere. Some local governments employ a consultant from a local business or university. In this case, a local government staff member should be assigned to act as liaison with the consultant.

Strategic planning has two time considerations—long-term and short-term. In the early stages of the planning process, participants look ahead and predit what may happen to the community over the long term, the next three to five years. Later, they will have to establish short-term strategies for moving in the direction the community wants to go over the next year.

A formal strategic planning process has the following results, each of which will be examined in future chapters (the long-term and short-term time considerations are evident here):

1. A mission statement for the organization
2. An environmental scan and conclusions about future scenarios in a three- to five-year period
3. Basic goals for the time period in the scan, and goals for the coming one-year period
4. Strategies and action steps that will move the organization toward the goals
5. Implementation plans that assign responsibilities for action steps.

These results are usually formalized in the written strategic plan; examples are found throughout this book and in its appendixes.

The process of formalizing a mission statement, forecasting scenarios, and setting goals for the organization will involve numerous meetings and other forums for the exchange of ideas. Participants in these forums should be representatives of all aspects of the community—elected and appointed officials, local government department heads and employees, business leaders, spokespersons for citizens' groups, members of boards and commissions. Deciding on action steps and detailing implementation plans are usually the responsibility of administrative and departmental staff.

The written plan generally goes through several drafts, with the final plan approved by the elected body. Once approved and published, the plan becomes a blueprint for action and decision-making as the local government moves toward its desired future.

What strategic planning is

As noted earlier, formal strategic planning in an organization must be regarded as a product and a process, both of which are valuable to an organization. As a process, planning is a means of prompting thought, provoking internal examination, and facilitating decision-making. In a local government setting, the process may include the identification of key persons who should be involved, or from whom input should be sought. This typically would include, in addition to those inside the government, others who have valuable information, key perceptions, or large bases of support.

Assembling such a diverse and potentially adversarial group may initially delay the process rather than facilitate it. However, it is better to invite and resolve conflict early in the discussion and decision-making stages than to confront it while trying to implement the resulting programs. In fact, diversity of perspective in the planning process frequently offers a significant benefit. A plan which is the result of debate and negotiation often represents a compromise in which opposing points of view have embraced an acceptable alternative.

The plan itself then becomes not only a compendium of program directions, philosophies, and strategies, but also a symbol of unity. The plan represents a collectively supported vision of a community's future and the most acceptable formula for allocating the always-scarce resources. This is particularly true as a local government begins to conduct formal strategic planning sessions for the first time.

For local governments that have used the process before, strategic planning becomes a style of organizational operation, a guide for decision-making, a "systematic means of coping with uncertainty,"[1] and a determinant of project feasibility and success. Finally, it can be a structure for long-term growth within which more immediate directions are highlighted. Thus, a three-year plan may describe the overall direction for an organization for the ensuing three-year period as well as determine the structure of the more imminent, one-year phase of the program.

A plan is a vision . . . a vision of the future and of what the community and its governing and management organizations can accomplish within the confines of future realities, as observed from the present.

What strategic planning is not

First and foremost, neither the process nor the product of strategic planning is a mechanism that relieves decision-makers of their ongoing responsibilities. Strategic planning defines the most likely conditions within which decisions must be made, and it can highlight the potential effects of various decisions. But it cannot prescribe specific courses of action. Given the best information, the best analysis and comprehension, and even the best luck, the plan can only refine our understanding of options. Final decisions will be made by individuals and groups who, even with the best information, remain human, and who must make difficult choices from opposing options. There is no guarantee that they will make the right selections. There is no guarantee that the data will remain constant or that conditions won't change. There is no guarantee that the programs designed to fit an accurately projected scenario of the future will succeed. The best conceived plans can fail. On the other hand, an organization that relies solely on intuitive decision-making can succeed. Although more informed decisions are possible through planning, and although the planning process enhances the chance of making the best decisions, it does not ensure success; it improves the chances.

Planning is not a panacea for resolving organizational or community conflicts. Although it may draw opposing factions closer through negotiation, it will not unite them, nor will it create consensus on philosophy or programming.

In communities where resources are scarce, strategic planning cannot increase them. It may be useful as a means of stretching resources, both human and capital. It can be an effective tool in reaching conclusions about which resources can have the most immediate impact when spent on problems or to take advantage of opportunities, but it cannot expand finite resources. However, the planning process *can* help to identify additional resources—state, federal, private, volunteer—and to maximize existing local resources.

As a process, strategic planning is not a one-time endeavor. It must be constant and ongoing. As the environment changes, or as our understanding of the environment becomes more clear, the plan can be amended and its resulting actions adjusted. The process must continue because the environment is always in flux. To plan once is to be unprepared. What was once flexibility becomes rigidity. To maintain flexibility, a community must constantly analyze the past, scrutinize the present, and prepare for the future.

One-time plans intended to serve as long-term community guides in the late 1980s might have failed to anticipate such dramatic events as the collapse of the Soviet Union, the unification of Germany, the depth of the economic recession in the United States, and the start and rapid conclusion of the Gulf War. They could not have accurately anticipated the massive layoffs of the early 1990s, the reduction in force of the U.S. armed services and the closure of military bases, reductions in federal defense procurement, or the extent of budget difficulties of federal and state governments resulting in their reduced allocations to local governments. The plans developed at the local level must be modified systematically to take such events into account.

In brief, planning must be regarded only as a means of facilitating decision-making and clarifying options. It cannot change the conditions of the environment and it cannot eliminate uncertainty. But it can create understanding, promote compromise, provide flexibility, and formulate a vision of the future and the best means of achieving it.

Pitfalls to avoid in strategic planning

As in any major organizational initiative, there are pitfalls in strategic planning. Awareness of some common faults in the process and product of strategic planning can help planners avoid some of them.

Regarding the plan as an end point   The first pitfall to avoid in strategic planning, which frequently occurs in organizations new to the planning process, is the inclination to regard the written plan as the end of the process. The plan—the product itself—is simply the structure resulting from examining potential opportunities and threats in the future environment. The greatest benefits of planning derive from the process: the discussions, analyses, and thought processes leading to decisions. Too often, plans are written, shelved, and forgotten. They must be disseminated to local interest groups, explained, and promoted if they are to be embraced and supported by those who will be expected to implement them and those who will be affected by them.

Regarding the plan as unalterable   A second pitfall to avoid is regarding the plan as unalterable. Plans and their analyses need to be reviewed constantly, and performance against planned goals and objectives requires constant and rigorous scrutiny. If conditions change, or if actual performance varies too much from the stated goals and objectives, local leaders need to assess why this is happening and decide how to react and what new programs to implement, targets to set, or resources to redistribute. To continue to pursue programs that are not proceeding as expected or objectives that are not being met only invites further divergence from plan to actual. As H. L. Mencken once admonished, "For every problem, there is a solution that is simple, neat, and wrong."[2] Continuous diligence can yield the right solutions at the right time.

Failing to question assumptions   Another frequent error is to permit preconceptions or other pre-established perspectives to be incorporated into plans without being thoroughly questioned. This often occurs when the source of that perspective is regarded as venerable or unimpeachable or is too highly placed in the organization to be questioned. Not challenging underlying assumptions, however, produces a plan which is no more than written justification for presumption. Within the local government context, for example, the ranking individual may be the city or county manager or an elected official. Such individuals often have superior ability to see the "big picture" but, because of the level of their responsibilities, may not see the details. Clerks and others who work on specific issues and programs, at lower organizational levels, probably do have this ability. Regrettably, their views are not always sought or, if they are, they may be disregarded because they are counter to assumptions held by persons at higher levels of the organization. Avoiding this pitfall of failing to question assumptions requires a conscious decision to solicit input from all levels and to accord all intelligence full consideration.

Failing to gain organizational commitment   Another pitfall, especially for organizations beginning strategic planning for the first time, is the lack of a full conceptual commitment to the process at all levels of the organization. As suggested earlier, it is vital that input be obtained from front line staff because of their perspectives and because it is they who will ultimately implement the programs prescribed by the plan and strive to achieve its goals and objectives. Middle managers must also provide input. One observer has noted: "The majority of managers in individual business units see little relation between what they do (and why they do it) and the corporate objectives and goals. This situation is what is best known as the "planning gap."[3] Involving individuals throughout the organization helps ensure their commitment. The most senior officials must also "buy in" to the process and communicate full support for the product. This sense of their commitment to the plan and to planning in general permeates all levels of the organization and generates further support for the goals and directions. Anything less than full support for the plan by the elected and senior appointed officials will be detected by program staff and constituents and will dilute the effectiveness of the programs. Anything less than enthusiasm for the process will be felt in subsequent planning cycles.

Adopting the wrong goals   Still another pitfall is the adoption of strategies which, while good ideas, might damage the organization's effectiveness. Strategic planners must be cautious in recommending only strategies which warrant taking the concomitant risks and which have the potential to be implemented. Public sector planners will do well to heed Jan Carlzon, president of Scandinavian Air Service, who wrote that the hardest thing to do in strategic planning is to abandon a good idea that doesn't fit the time or place.[4]

When a local government or one of its departments embarks on a course of action for which it has insufficient funding, knowledge, experience, or political support, it loses its capacity for quality performance not only in the new program, but also in existing programs. Overextending can cause disastrous misallocations of resources and embarrassing conflicts. Many a business has become too diversified, and the same can happen to a local government that attempts to resolve all of its community's ills too quickly. The wiser approach to planning is to do a few things well and to move forward in small measures. For a local government, public safety, public works, education, human services, and essential infrastructure often form the first tier of responsibility. As resources become available to provide more than these essential levels of service, good ideas can be investigated and implemented.

Local governments and their planners might keep in mind the lament of Charles de Gaulle: "How can anyone rule a country that

produces 265 varieties of cheese?"[5] Given the diversity of local services and demands, planners must be alert for inconsistencies among
individual elements of a plan. The various components of a total plan
"are not always directly related to one another and can even work at
cross purposes."[6]

Imposing unnecessary limitations   All of these potential pitfalls
apply both to public entities and to private businesses. There is another pitfall which occurs more often in the public sector. It is not
unusual for local government organizations to become confined in
their thinking because of various limits on them. The breadth of local operations is often well defined in law, ordinance, regulation, or
originating charter. A business, given adequate capacity, resources,
and motivation, can try new markets or product lines. It can sell
unprofitable divisions, close some plants, or shut down operations
entirely. Such alternatives are not available to the public sector. Another limit on local governments is lack of funding, which impedes
change even when decision-makers are motivated and prepared to
implement new strategies. This lack of resources may to lead to viewing the appropriate future course of action as "business as usual." This
attitude may be appropriate if it refers to the scope of operations, but
it should not be the approach to seeking means of providing services.
Local governments can strive to approach old problems with new
solutions and to perform ongoing tasks in innovative and more efficient ways. These strategies will be the result of strategic planning.

1. Jan Carlzon, *Moments of Truth*
    (New York: Ballinger Publish-
    ing Company, 1987).
2. *The Oxford Dictionary of Quo-
    tations,* 3rd ed. (Oxford: Oxford
    University Press, 1980), p. 173.
3. Cass Bettinger, "Use Corporate
    Culture to Trigger High
    Performance," *Journal of
    Business Strategy* 10, no. 2
    (March/April 1989) 38–42.
4. Carlzon, *Moments of Truth,*
    p. 55.
5. *Oxford Dictionary of Quota-
    tions,* p. 173.
6. Peter M. Scott and Walter W.
    Simpson "Connecting Overall
    Corporate Planning to Indi-
    vidual Business Units," *Public
    Utilities Fortnightly* 123, no. 12
    (June 8, 1987): 27.

Chapter 2

The Strategic Plan: Analysis

In discussing the elements of a strategic plan, a note of caution is important. The reader of this text should be aware that the concepts involved have varying labels. For example, where one plan uses the terms *goals, objectives,* and *strategies,* another might express the same concepts as the *vision, targets,* and *action steps.* Where this book uses the term *environmental scan,* a strategic plan for the city of Arlington, Texas, used the term *alternative approaches* for viewing future environments. What is referred to in this text as goals, objectives, and strategies were referred to in that city's plan as *recommended solutions. Funding consideration* in that plan corresponded to *implementation plan* in this text. *Stakeholders* can be called *role players. Environmental scans* can be called *needs assessments* or *SWOT analyses* (SWOT is an acronym for "strengths, weaknesses, opportunities, and threats"). There is no consistent usage in either the professional or the academic literature. To become preoccupied with the terminology is to be distracted from the actual meaning. The reader should consider concepts, however they are labeled.

Local government and its stakeholders

"Stakeholder" is a term that has evolved in the literature on strategic planning and in other fields. It refers to persons who have a direct interest in what is done by an organization.

For a business, the stakeholders are typically the owners, the managers and employees, the vendors and distributors, and the customers. For a local government, the list will include the following at the very least:

1. Elected officials
    a. Local elected officials
    b. Relevant federal and state elected officials
    c. Elected officials of other local jurisdictions

2. Other officials
    a. Senior local government professional managers
    b. Other local government managers
    c. All other local government employees
    d. Members of boards, commissions, and other appointed groups
    e. Federal and state officials with oversight responsibilities
    f. Key staff members and advisors of elected officials and all of the above

3. Recipients and users of public services
    a. Homeowners and other residents who use basic local services (public works, public safety, and so on)
    b. Users of public facilities such as parks, libraries, courts, and transportation systems
    c. Teachers, other education officials, and students
    d. Public support recipients and those in need of public support
    e. Special interest groups with particular needs

4. Other organizations and individuals
    a. Businesses and business organizations
    b. Employees of constituent businesses, whether residents or not
    c. Local colleges and universities
    d. Nonprofit organizations located in or providing services to the jurisdiction
    e. Operators of public facilities such as beaches, airports, train or bus stations
    f. Operators and users of cultural outlets such as museums, theaters, and historical sites
    g. Leaders and congregations of churches, synagogues, other places of worship
    h. Commanders of military bases and those who are stationed or employed there
    i. Travelers to and through the area.

Businesses must constantly decide where or how to expand, contract, seek new opportunity, or change operations; so must local governments. As they do so, planners in both sectors must receive input from and consider the effect on their stakeholders.

A difference for the public sector, of course, is that the decisions will ultimately be reached at the highest elected levels. For localities, this means city councils and county boards. Unlike the business strategic planner, whose sole or primary consideration is which combinations of goods and services will generate the maximum financial return, the public planner must be aware of different dynamics. Decision-makers in the public sector generally feel obligated to various constituencies among the community's stakeholders. They are driven by values of public service unlike the values that drive business decisions. Thus, some decisions will require resources for political or even emotional reasons. Some may fly in the face of logic based entirely on financial reasoning. Some sections of town may require revitalization or beautification. Some areas may have a lower need than others for infrastructure development or other services but may in fact receive greater consideration for scarce resource allocation because of the need to demonstrate official commitment to all areas of the community and all elements of the population.

It is important for strategic planners to be cognizant of the dynamics of such decision-making both in general and within the specific local context. It may even behoove those responsible for the plan to hold early, informal discussions with key decision-makers in order to identify such possibilities and determine whether to address them in the plan. In any event, planning and program implementation in the political environment cannot reflect simple cost-benefit analyses alone. Since the plans and programs will reflect some political and emotional factors, the architects of the plan must be prepared and instructed in these matters.

Those who manage the strategic planning process for local governments should solicit and coordinate input from stakeholders efficiently and systematically, identify various levels of involvement for all of the potential participants, keep all interested parties informed of progress, solicit and incorporate feedback, develop and gauge support and opposition, and propose and encourage compromise.

In the environmental scan, it is important to be aware of the plans of others. This is especially true for a city or town where there is a single major employer, such as a college or university, a military base, or a major corporation. In such areas, advance knowledge of expansions, plant or base closures, relocations, or even new product lines will help planners better understand the environmental forces that will shape the future of their community.

In cities or towns like these, it is critical to involve the other organization's senior officials in the process of public planning. While this may seem self-evident, there are numerous examples of poor "town-gown," military-civilian, or corporate-civic relations. Such groups are important stakeholders just as are the other elements of the community.

Stakeholder involvement in larger, more diverse communities requires similar but broader representation in the planning process. For example, a few business representatives might represent the entire business community; rather than representing their specific businesses, they might be agents of the local Chamber of Commerce. Other umbrella organizations might also represent a larger constituency of citizens, schools, or other stakeholders.

Stakeholders in an internal strategic plan

An exception to the inclusive approach may occur when strategic planning is designed with the specific intent of taking an inward look at local government and its services. Often, such planning is expedient as a first step to set the agenda for future, broader planning efforts. In such cases, it is the senior city or county staff which takes part in the process. The accompanying sidebar shows the structure of the Wichita, Kansas, Strategic Agenda Coordinating Committee and Subcommittees.

Strategic Agenda Coordinating Committee
  Assistant City Manager
  Management Intern
  Training Director
  Director of Public Works
  Wichita State University
  Director of Parks
  Chief Planner

Strategic Issue Subcommittees

Community Enhancement Subcommittee
  Director of Parks
  Assistant to the City Manager
  Chief Planner
  Director of Planning
  Director of Libraries
  Housing Director
  Director of Health

Economic Development Subcommittee
  Director of Finance
  Industrial Development Specialist

Communities involve their stakeholders in differing ways. Some communities prefer a grass-roots approach and heavily involve citizens in the strategic planning process. This can be an effective means of planning, which creates greater legitimacy for the resulting goals, objectives, and strategies. Whitley County, Indiana, in its strategic plan, recognized the value of obtaining participation from its component cities in its process. Its strategy committee included representation from the communities of Columbia City, Churubusco, Larwill, and South Whitley. The first goal in the Whitley County plan reflects the need for input from those important stakeholders:

Director of Airports
Acting Director of Economic Development
Wichita State University
Century II/Expo Hall Director

Governmental Coordination and Image Subcommittee
Chief Planner
Citizen Participation Coordinator
Training Director
Fire Chief
Citizen Rights and Services Director
Superintendent of Central Inspection
Public Information Officer

Government Structure and Finance Subcommittee
Assistant City Manager
Management Intern
Controller
Financial Analyst
Internal Auditor
Energy Resources Director
Director of Law
Personnel Director

Infrastructure Management Subcommittee
Director of Public Works
Assistant to the Public Works Director
Director of Emergency Communications
Maintenance Engineer
City Engineer
Chief Planner
MTA General Manager
Chief Engineer, Water

"Elimination of duplicated, segmented, inefficient County, City, and Town services . . . a business approach to taxation."

Other local government strategic planning efforts include input from their stakeholders through organizations representing larger groups of individuals. For example, the strategic planning process for Catawba County, North Carolina, included the component municipal governments, three local school boards, the Chamber of Commerce, the League of Women Voters, political parties, the operator of the local airport, developers, arts organizations, and teachers. The authors of the planning document subsequently acknowledged the benefit of this broad-based stakeholder involvement as transforming the process from one started by government officials to one "owned" by the entire community. Government was characterized as the catalyst. The long-term result was anticipated to be new roles for stakeholders throughout the community and new relationships with various governmental units.

The text of local government strategic plans often states explicitly that the process needs to belong to the stakeholders in a community rather than to elected officials or to the local government organization. The latter is sometimes perceived as being controlling, short-term in its thinking, too closely tied to budgets, or even in an ivory tower and out-of-touch. The preferred approach to local area strategic planning is consensus from the community, the local government organization, and local elected officials.

Is it important to have a broad range of input into a community's strategic planning process? It may be. Strategic planners must decide who to involve, how to involve them, and how to solicit input from those who are not directly involved. It will and ought to be different everywhere.

The growing importance of stakeholder input into the process is evident. Increased citizen communication with local governments can be measured to demonstrate the growing interest of citizen stakeholders in the planning and management of their communities. An Arlington, Texas, plan illustrated the increase in the number of calls received by the local government's public information officer (see Figure 2.1). Even if this dramatic increase is partly explained by population growth, it suggests a significant level of citizen involvement in planning for the future of their community.

In addition to determining how to ensure the optimum input for everyone and for every group, those who organize the planning process must also consider the most efficient size and composition of the planning group and the type of group process to employ for gathering information. This will be discussed in Chapter 5, "Organizational Considerations."

The inherent beliefs of an organization

The inherent beliefs and values of the most influential members of an organization help structure planning and other activities. They are what Michael Kami refers to as "psychographics and aspirations."[1] These beliefs are so ingrained in individuals as to be unidentifiable to them personally or to their colleagues. However, the awareness of such beliefs by those involved in strategic planning is critical. Planners must recognize the importance of these beliefs and attempt to identify and comprehend them. Often this means knowing the point of view of top officials who may not even be involved in the planning deliberations.

Much research has been devoted to identifying the inherent beliefs of organizations. Of course, they are not easy to define. The seminal study is *In Search of Excellence*, in which Peters and Waterman highlight seven "values" usually found in "excellent" companies:

- a belief in being the best
- a belief in the importance of attention to detail
- a belief in the importance of the individual
- a belief in superior quality and service
- a belief in innovation and the willingness to support failure
- a belief in the importance of informality to enhance communication
- a belief in the importance of economic growth and profit.[2]

The fourth of these points—an orientation to service—tends to be more prevalent in the municipal workforce than in business. Consider the following array of values identified in one municipality's plan:

- a strong commitment to manage change
- the pursuit of a sense of identity and character of the locale
- a commitment to neighborliness, friendliness, and a warm civic personality
- the fostering of neighborhood initiatives and local leadership

Year	No. of calls	Increase over previous year	% Increase
1	66,400	—	—
2	74,916	8,516	12.8
3	93,408	18,492	24.6
4	136,506	43,098	46.1

Figure 2.1. Calls received by the public information officer, Arlington, Texas.

- the encouraging of respect for and enjoyment of diverse cultures; pluralism; social tolerance; and integration in neighborhoods, housing, the workplace, and recreation.

One municipality's basic premises may reflect concern for the diversity of the local economy; high standards of quality in urban design, construction, and community appearance; close coordination between the public and private sectors; and maintaining the richness of the area's traditions, values, and history. Another locale may recognize the need to grow while preserving the way of life cherished by the community. Such values as friendliness; conservation; and enjoyment of the environment, arts, culture, and history reflect a need for strategies intended to change some things while preserving others.

The elements of the underlying beliefs of an organization have been summarized in various ways. One such classification includes

- attitudes toward change
- degree of consensus between senior officials
- standards and values
- concern for people
- attitudes toward openness and communication
- conflict resolution style (i.e., win/lose versus win/win)
- group orientation toward the market, the consumer
- excitement, pride, "esprit de corps"
- commitment
- teamwork.[3]

In the public sector, the guiding principles of an organization will manifest themselves in legislation and public policy. At the local level, they will affect the types of public works and infrastructure, libraries and parks, educational systems, public safety, and other public services citizens enjoy. Both the senior policy-makers and those beneath them who implement the programs hold inherent beliefs that are reflected collectively in the quality of their services. Local government leaders and employees may vary in their attitudes toward change, preferences for small town or rural life-style, spirit of cooperation, respect for all members of the community, and styles of leadership. If the individuals' beliefs are consistent with the philosophy and intent of the plan, the operations stand a better chance of achieving success.

Planners need to understand the degree to which a general philosophical consensus exists among key elected and appointed officials. If change is necessary, should it be incremental of more massive? Is there an acceptance of business or residential growth, fiscal conservatism, the need to support all segments of the jurisdiction's population? As public sector planners consider new strategies, they must understand the collective will to accept change, whether slow or dramatic. This understanding can help them clarify goals and objectives before allocating resources.

Collective values, standards of behavior, and perceptions of human needs affect the manner in which programs are selected and targets identified. The local government planner should be aware of the operating styles of the community's leaders and their attitudes toward seeking compromise, open and regular communication, and commitment to the public welfare.

Understanding these factors will not dictate the direction a community will set or which programs will be funded. It will, however, illuminate the context within which those decisions will be made. It may help to identify where compromises may be feasible. In the current vernacular, in order to know where you're going, it is vital to understand "where you're coming from."

Appendix 1 shows how one jurisdiction's plan, that of Santa Clarita, California, illustrates both the process and the product of determining a community's inherent beliefs.

The mission statement

The mission statement of an organization reflects its essential purpose—its "raison d'etre." For this reason, it should seldom change. Mission statements, though not always labeled as such, can be found in any number of documents. They may be referred to as the organization's corporate vision, its purpose, or its objective.

In the private sector, statements for businesses may be found in originating charters, annual reports, or stockholder communications. Such essential descriptions of a company's purpose tend to focus on profits, commercial leadership, return on investment, market share, and quality service.

In the public sector, mission statements can be found in municipal charters, annual budgets, policy documents and long-term planning records. Many such statements have a common theme: to provide the maximum quality and quantity of public services to the taxpayers and other constituents at the lowest tax rate possible. The statements in the plans of Cocoa, Florida, and Berkley, Michigan, illustrate this similarity. Cocoa: "To provide for the health, comfort, safety, and convenience of the citizens of Cocoa." Berkley: "To provide public services and enlightened leadership to the residents of Berkley by the most efficient, effective, equitable, economical, and democratic means possible."

Such statements should be concise but encompassing enough to withstand the changes wrought by time and shifts in critical environmental factors. The importance of being concise and specific in the mission statement cannot be overemphasized. Tregoe and Tobia have addressed this need. If you were a manager who had to make

Text continues on page 26.

Environmental scanning

The following future scenarios were considered by the International City/County Management Association's FutureVisions Consortium, which conducted a scan of factors that will affect local government management in the 1990s:

The information revolution will enable staff to perform new functions or provide services more effectively, but it also increases the time needed to reach decisions and creates important organizational development issues.

The rate of technological change promises to astonish.

The shift from representative to participatory democracy heralds an unprecedented degree of citizen involvement in governmental decision making.

Local governments face problems that cannot be addressed by single jurisdictions; our future depends on comprehensive solutions to issues that range from transportation, solid waste management, and air quality control to drugs, homelessness, and poverty.

Consensus on community goals is increasingly important; failure to achieve consensus often stands in the way of achieving future visions.

In the next twenty years, economically underdeveloped nations will produce 200 million new workers, while the United States faces a continuing labor shortage. At the same time, the United States will gain significantly in number of elderly adults. By 2020, 17% of the U.S. population will be over 65; and by 2030, 21% will be over 65. The number of "elderly elderly" is also growing rapidly. In 1985, there were 2.1 million people age 85 or older, a number that is expected to more than double to 4.9 million by 2000 and to reach 6.6 million by 2010.

The consequences of poor education and training go beyond those associated with the labor supply. There are direct correlations between failure to complete high school and criminal activity, unemployment, dependence on welfare, and other social problems.

Cultural, racial, ethnic, and gender diversity will continue to grow across the country, bringing managers opportunities and challenges in their organizations and their communities.

Global competition will determine which U.S. jobs and products can hold their own in the world economy. Local governments can expect federal cutbacks to continue, although mandates and regulations will continue to expand.

As the private sector provides more services traditionally provided by local government, the distinctions between the private and public sectors are blurring. As the opportunities for joint development and sharing of risks expand, local governments will need to be especially vigilant on questions of ethics, accountability, and equitable access to services.

Citizens have become accustomed to good service and quick response from private-sector businesses, and they are coming to expect the same from local government.

Continuing concern about environmental issues is an aspect of broader concerns about health, well-being, and quality of life. Debate will continue about strategy, process, cost, technology, and results, and the local government manager will play a greater role in managing and enforcing environmental regulations.

Local governments will be forced to spend more time, energy, and resources on health issues—both as employers and as providers of health services. By the year 2000, abusers of alcohol, drugs, and cigarettes will make up an estimated 50% of all hospital admissions. Until a cure is found, the number of AIDS patients will continue to escalate. By 2000, children born to teenagers will constitute 15% of all births in the United States. Finally, the aging population will place increasing demands on the health services system.

The organization, staffing, equipping, training, and financing of local police services will be dominated by ongoing debates about the most effective strategies for dealing with crime, substance abuse, social unrest, cultural diversity (in the community and on the police force), terrorism, and burnout among police officers. The most dramatic changes will come in the area of technology· portable computers, weapons that permit officers to stop individuals without lethal force, and increasingly sophisticated forensics techniques.

Communities in the future will place even greater value on leisure services than they do today. They will need an up-to-date, well-managed leisure service infrastructure coupled with responsive, diverse, relevant, and satisfying programs.

Trends such as declining average household size, increasing median age, and increasing numbers of single-parent families indicate that housing needs and preferences will continue to evolve during the next decade. The decline in four-bedroom colonials will be offset by an increase in one- and two-bedroom homes, clustered closer to each other as well as to services and transportation.

The link between economic vitality and continued infrastructure improvement has been fully established, and the future depends on a commitment to finance infrastructure maintenance and improvements.

Source: "Future Challenges, Future Opportunities: The Final Report of the ICMA FutureVisions Consortium, *Public Management*, July 1991, center insert.

decisions about product, market positioning and allocating resources, they ask, what guidance would you get from this plank in the strategy of one major U.S. company?: "Our business is the creation of machine and methods to help find solutions to the increasingly complex problems of business, government, science, space exploration, education, medicine, and nearly every other area of human endeavor."[4]

The ability to be quickly scanned and understood is important in a mission statement. Equally vital is that a mission statement be enduring. As will be discussed in a later chapter, an organization's goals and objectives must be sensitive to environmental factors to permit flexibility and response to changing threats and opportunities. This all takes place, however, within the context of a constant mission. Businesses still seek maximum profits and return on investments. Public bodies still wish to provide the highest quality services possible at the lowest possible tax rate.

Changes in mission statements may occur when a major event takes place. For a business, this may occur when a company enters a new market or when a whole industry is deregulated. For a public body, major changes occur infrequently. One such change, however, might be the incorporation of a new area into the jurisdiction that substantially alters the composition and needs of the community. In the case of such a significant change, the mission statement may require amendment.

The mission statement communicates the organization's purpose to a variety of audiences and forms the basis for goals, objectives, and implementation plans. The existence of a clearly communicated mission can allow employees and other stakeholders to stretch to reach new heights without losing sight of the principles on which the community was founded or has historically operated.

Environmental scanning
Any organization exists and operates in environments that affect its ability to be successful. Organizations try to picture the future environmental context within which goals and objectives will be set and strategies implemented. They must anticipate as nearly as possible what will occur in the future and construct their plan in a manner consistent with the most likely scenarios.

Their planning will be complicated by the fact that environmental factors undergo constant change. Unemployment rises and falls, demographics shift, and federal and state dollars available for programs at the local level may be increased or, more likely, reduced. Not only do these factors change, but they may do so in unpredictable ways. Furthermore, the future may be affected by new, completely unanticipated factors, such as the collapse of the Soviet Union and the subsequent reduction in federal defense procurement. Strategic planning enables an organization to cope better with such fluctuations and to take maximum advantage of such changes.

An organization's environment has several concurrent contexts. There is the organizational context, the factors which exist within the organization itself. External contexts include the industry (in this case, the practice of public administration) and a geographic context (city or county, state, region, nation, or global). Because of these multiple contexts, the impact of environmental change frequently tends to be more exponential than arithmetic. For this reason, planners sometimes use computer programs to assist in scanning to determine their future needs.

The process of environmental scanning is the same for a public agency as for a profit-making business. Whereas a business will scan the environment for factors affecting its ability to make a profit, a public agency will be concerned with tax revenues and changes requiring new patterns of resource allocation.

The breadth of environmental factors to scan in each community will be extensive, although the content will vary considerably. The Berkley, Michigan, scan is illustrated in Appendix 2 simply by listing a portion of the plan's table of contents.

The scanning matrix   There are numerous models to follow in reviewing the several environments within which planning and program operations will occur. These are merely tools to facilitate the scanning process; they may or may not actually appear in the final written document. One type of scanning matrix cited in business-oriented strategic planning literature is illustrated in Figure 2.2. It is applicable for local government planning as well.

At the top of the matrix in Figure 2.2, identified by letters, are the various environments in which a community may operate and plan:

A. Internal (the local government organization)
B. Public administration (trends in public management generally)
C. Local (the community)
D. Regional
E. State
F. National
G. Global.

At the left is a list of environmental factors to be considered in creating a local government's strategic plan:

1. Economic and financial
2. Demographic

3. Technological
4. Legal and regulatory
5. Social and cultural
6. Competitive
7. Managerial
8. Physical and environmental
9. Other.

The matrix can be used to list factors that are important in each environment. For reference, each "cell" in the matrix is labeled with the appropriate letter and number.

The matrix illustrated in Figure 2.2 is designed to be very general. Cities and counties will have numerous environments to scan under the various headings. Some factors will be unique to a community; for example, a community may need to consider the future activities of a major local corporation, university, or public facility such as an airport. These and other environments should be represented by stakeholders who participate in the planning process. The matrix will provide direction for those planners conducting the scans of the various environments. The review and assessment of each scan can then take place within the context of the other areas noted in the matrix. Structuring the scanning process in this way permits an orderly review.

	Environments			
Factors	**Internal** **A**	**Public admini- stration B**	**Local** **C**	**Regional** **D**
1–Economic and financial	A-1	B-1	C-1	D-1
2–Demographic	A-2	B-2	C-2	D-2
3–Technological	A-3	B-3	C-3	D-3
4–Legal and regulatory	A-4	B-4	C-4	D-4
5–Social and cultural	A-5	B-5	C-5	D-5
6–Competitive	A-6	B-6	C-6	D-6
7–Managerial	A-7	B-7	C-7	D-7
8–Physical and environmental	A-8	B-8	C-8	D-8
9–Other	A-9	B-9	C-9	D-9

Figure 2.2. Environmental scanning matrix.

It is helpful to conduct the scan as a two-step process. The first step is to consider each cell in the matrix and list the relevant points to be considered. The second is to extract the opportunities and threats in summary fashion. Some cells may not be relevant to future goals and objectives, or the relevant information may already appear in another cell. This does not matter. It is simply important that all pertinent information receive full consideration. Because public bodies often have a broad range of functions and responsbilities, the matrix can become large and cluttered as all conceivable factors are listed. Some of the items local governments will need to consider in the environmental scan are listed in Figure 2.3. The list is intended to suggest the type of intelligence that is relevant to strategic planning; it is not intended to be all-inclusive or to suggest that all this information must be compiled.

Local government planners must carefully consider the factors to be analyzed. The environmental scan is the basis for better understanding the future. With it, planners can determine the best goals, objectives, and strategies possible with given resources.

To show how the process works, later chapters will build on the example shown in Figure 2.3. The environmental factors listed here will be used as the basis for sample goals, objectives, strategies, and implementation plans.

Text continues on page 38.

Factors	Environments		
	State E	National F	Global G
1–Economic and financial	E-1	F-1	G-1
2–Demographic	E-2	F-2	G-2
3–Technological	E-3	F-3	G-3
4–Legal and regulatory	E-4	F-4	G-4
5–Social and cultural	E-5	F-5	G-5
6–Competitive	E-6	F-6	G-6
7–Managerial	E-7	F-7	G-7
8–Physical and environmental	E-8	F-8	G-8
9–Other	E-9	F-9	G-9

Figure 2.2. Continued

Internal environment

Economic and financial factors (A-1)

1. Trends in local revenues, including taxes and fees
2. Status of federal and state assistance
3. Availability of private grants
4. Trends in expenditure levels, service demands, and transfer payments
5. Programs of business attraction and job development
6. Cost of contractual services and procured goods
7. Debt service and municipal bond rating
8. Performance of investment portfolio
9. Trends in benefits costs and liability expenditures
10. Accuracy of annual revenue and expenditure projections
11. Status of local user fees for public services and development actions, and their potential revenue opportunities

Demographic factors (A-2)

1. Number of employees by classification, skill level, and tenure
2. Composition of governmental workforce by grade, cross-tabulated by age, race, and sex
3. Number of employees eligible or near-eligible for retirement

Technological factors (A-3)

1. State of computer and other technology in the local government
2. Areas where resources could be saved through technological advances, and the costs associated with doing so
3. Areas where technology will be replaced or upgraded
4. Skills likely to be in demand by the local government in the future, and the gap between the present and future
5. Technological advances in other localities

Legal and regulatory factors (A-4)

1. Federal and state regulations or laws which will affect the availability of local resources
2. Legislation or regulations at any level that will facilitate progress, permit taking advantage of opportunities, or avoid threats to the success of the plan
3. Federal and state legislators and officials with influence in law-making, and whether they are accessible and supportive

Social and cultural factors (A-5)

1. Extent to which staff and programs reflect the social and cultural composition of the community

Figure 2.3. Environmental factors to consider in strategic planning.

Competitive factors (A-6)

1. Federal, state, and private grants available to local government on a competitive basis
2. Local grants and other resources for which the local government has applied
3. Comparative advantages and disadvantages of this community over other communities with similar needs and assets and with which the local government must compete for resources

Managerial factors (A-7)

1. Strengths and weaknesses of management staff
2. Status of succession plans
3. Alignment of current managerial talent and structure with future programs and needs
4. Areas in which management training could be beneficial

Physical and environmental factors (A-8)

1. Infrastructure in place, location and costs of needed new construction, and costs of replacing or maintaining existing facilities
2. Local issues of commercial or residential development
3. Concerns of local conservationists and environmentalists with respect to wildlife preservation and air and water pollution

Public administration environment

Economic and financial factors (B-1)

1. Trends in federal and state funding for local programs
2. Performance of municipal bonds and other funds

Demographic factors (B-2)

1. Availability of recent graduates with degrees in public administration, political science, and other skills in demand by local governments

Technological factors (B-3)

1. New computer or other technological applications for local government functions

Legal and regulatory factors (B-4)

1. Issues being followed by the International City/County Management Association (ICMA), the National League of Cities (NLC), the National Association of Counties (NACo), the American Society for Public Administration (ASPA), and other

Figure 2.3. Continued

organizations representing local governments or those who
work for or with them
2. Legal issues and decisions in other jurisdictions with potential
local implications
3. Trends in other localities toward the imposition of user fees for
selected public services and facilities
4. Trends in other localities toward the imposition of developer
taxes

Social and cultural factors (B-5)

Not applicable

Competitive factors (B-6)

1. Comparative tax rates for businesses and residents which
make the community more attractive than other localities

Managerial factors (B-7)

1. Management issues identified by professional associations in
the field of public administration and the specific professional
and technical areas of local government
2. Management issues being followed by professional organizations in the field of general management

Physical and environmental factors (B-8)

1. Status of air and water pollution, development and land use,
and other environmental issues affecting other local governments
2. Positions of other local governments and pending legislation
and legal decisions
3. Costs associated with environmental issues and resolutions

Local environment

Economic and financial factors (C-1)

1. Key local economic indicators, including employment, job
growth, and consumer confidence
2. Patterns of, and reasons for, business attraction, retention, or
loss
3. Jurisdictional, residential, and business growth patterns
afffecting demand for local public services
4. Such growth patterns contributing to the locality's tax
revenues
5. Positions of local Chambers of Commerce and other business
organizations

Figure 2.3. Continued

Demographic factors (C-2)

1. Migration in and out of the jurisdiction
2. Data for the area as a whole and by neighborhood (including cross-tabulations) with respect to age, sex, race, education level, income level, family size, and literacy rates
3. Number of persons for whom English is a second language
4. Changing patterns in the nature and quantity of current and future service delivery

Technological factors (C-3)

Not applicable

Legal and regulatory factors (C-4)

Not applicable

Social and cultural factors (C-5)

1. Special social and cultural needs of sub-populations
2. Existing social and cultural services or events
3. Inter-cultural conflicts
4. Crime statistics and patterns

Competitive factors (C-6)

Not applicable

Managerial factors (C-7)

1. Strength and structure of the community leadership

Physical and environmental factors (C-8)

1. Comparative appearance of, and access of public services to, neighborhoods
2. Infrastructural needs of various parts of the jurisdiction
3. Downtown or other areas requiring revitalization
4. Historic buildings or areas and cultural and recreational facilities which require up-keep
5. Historic, cultural, and recreational areas which represent opportunities to attract tourism or to initiate beneficial programs

Regional environment

Economic and social factors (D-1)

1. Local share of costs of inter-jurisdictional systems for mass transportation, waste disposal, parks and recreation, power and utilities, and other public services

Figure 2.3. Continued

2. Patterns of, and reasons for, business attraction, loss, and retention in the region
3. Effect of weather and climate on attracting local business
4. Regional residential and business growth patterns as they will affect demand for regional public services

Demographic factors (D-2)

1. Migration in and out of the region
2. Regional data with respect to age, sex, race, education level, income level, family size, and literacy rates
3. Changing population patterns and significant distinctions between the region and its component localities

Technological factors (D-3)

1. State of technology for providing power and other regional public services
2. Costs to localities of upgrading existing technology for providing regional public services

Legal and regulatory factors (D-4)

1. Status of legal conflicts and other legal matters between jurisdictions

Social and cultural factors (D-5)

1. Cultural distinctions and conflicts among jurisdictions within the region
2. Crime statistics and patterns in the region

Competitive factors (D-6)

1. Competition for business attraction and expansion and tourism revenues among jurisdictions within the region
2. Existing and potential regional approaches to business attraction

Managerial factors (D-7)

1. Need for and management of regional boards, authorities, and commissions to provide or manage public services

Physical and environmental factors (D-8)

1. Existing and needed inter-jurisdictional environmental programs, services, or facilities
2. Environmental policies and practices of one jurisdiction as they affect neighboring jurisdictions

Figure 2.3. Continued

State environment

Economic and financial factors (E-1)

1. Patterns in and projections for state revenues, spending, and appropriations to localities
2. Projections for funding of existing or new state agencies, programs, or services affecting the locality
3. Pending or forthcoming state tax legislation or policies that will affect local businesses or residents
4. Statewide patterns of, and policies affecting, business attraction, retention, and expansion

Demographic factors (E-2)

1. Changing demographic patterns and relative distinctions among the locality, the region, and the state

Technological factors (E-3)

1. Nature of technology used by the state to provide public services as it affects the locality and its constituents

Legal and regulatory factors (E-4)

1. Current or needed state legislation or legal actions that will affect the operations of local government or the lives of its constituents

Social and cultural factors (E-5)

1. Cultural distinctions and conflicts among jurisdictions within the state
2. Conflicts between the more and less urbanized areas of the state

Competitive factors (E-6)

1. Equality of state services and funding to competing areas
2. State competitiveness for federal funding and services

Managerial factors (E-7)

1. Management of state agencies and operations affecting the local government and its constituents
2. Capabilities and performance of local representatives to the state legislature
3. Capabilities and performance of statewide elected officials and employees

Figure 2.3. Continued

Physical and environmental factors (E-8)
1. State practices and policies and existing, pending, or needed legislation concerning the environment, infrastructure, or public facilities, as they affect the locality and its constituents

National environment

Economic and financial factors (F-1)

1. Trends in, and projections for, federal expenditures to state and local governments or for programs that affect the state or the locality
2. Trends in relevant key indicators, including inflation, interest rates, business patterns, growth in the GNP, consumer confidence, and spending and saving patterns
3. Federal support and assistance for business programs to export goods or services

Demographic factors (F-2)

1. National trends, legislation, and policies regarding immigration as they affect the locality

Technological factors (F-3)

Not applicable

Legal and regulatory factors (F-4)

1. Status of current or needed legislation or policies that will affect the specific locality and its constituents

Social and cultural factors (F-5)

Not applicable

Competitive factors (F-6)

1. State's effectiveness in competing for federal funds and services
2. Locality's ability to compete for federal funding and services
3. Future of federal employment in the locality and the region

Managerial factors (F-7)

1. Effectiveness of state and local elected officials as advocates at the federal level
2. Performance of federal agencies and officials affecting the locality

Physical and environmental factors (F-8)

1. Proximity of, and laws and regulations pertaining to, federal parks and other facilities

Figure 2.3. Continued

2. Proximity of military bases and other federal facilities and the potential for their closure or expansion, and the effects thereof
3. Current or needed federal legislation or regulations concerning pollution, airport noise standards, land conservation, wildlife protection, and other environmental concerns affecting the locality

Global environment

Economic and financial factors (G-1)

1. Financial stability of countries to which local businesses either directly or indirectly export goods or services or from which they import goods or services
2. Opportunities to initiate new export and import programs
3. Relevant economic indicators, including the balance of trade and exchange rates
4. Opportunities to attract U.S. operations of foreign-owned businesses

Demographic factors (G-2)

Not applicable

Technological factors (G-3)

Not applicable

Legal and regulatory factors (G-4)

1. Current and needed federal policies to protect local industries
2. Current and proposed laws of other nations near the locality as they might affect the locality and its constituents
3. Pertinent international law and practices affecting the locality and its constituents
4. U.S. border regulations where localities are near international borders

Social and cultural factors (G-5)

1. Social and cultural conflicts of localities near international borders

Competitive factors (G-6)

Not applicable

Managerial factors (G-7)

Not applicable

Physical and environmental factors (G-8)

Not applicable

Figure 2.3. Continued

The internal scan   An environmental scan is frequently divided into an *external* scan, in which strategic planners view the world "out there," and an *internal* scan, in which they examine the strengths and weaknesses of the organization itself. The external scan is often easier; many communities are adept at studying facts. The internal scan, however, involves intangible political and emotional factors in addition to economic and demographic considerations.

One important component of an internal scan is the community's perception of the government and its services. A city or county can go a long way in the accurate assessment of community attitudes by conducting interviews and surveys. These need not be elaborate or expensive, although as communities grow and issues become broader and more complex, such surveys do tend to be more formal and detailed.

A citizen attitude survey can reveal valuable information about local preferences. Two or more surveys can demonstrate patterns in choices and shifts in attitudes. Berkley, Michigan, hired an independent consultant to conduct two surveys six years apart. Questions were asked about the types of municipal services and people's perceptions of their neighborhoods, levels of participation in events, and more.

The planners in Berkley learned that resident approval of municipal services was high. They determined that citizen satisfaction with city services had not declined over the six-year period between the two surveys. One question in the survey related to the willingness of Berkley's residents to pay for public improvements. Results showed that from 1981 to 1987, willingness to pay for street reconstruction and resurfacing increased from 12.0% to 22.2%. Other areas where respondents showed increased willingness to pay included improved street lighting (12% to 23.9%), tree planting and landscaping (14% to 33.4%), and park improvements (12% to 25.7%).

This information is invaluable for strategic planners. The community's expenditures can be aligned with the areas for which there is a willingness to pay. Conversely, choices between competing demands for scarce resources may become more clear to local decision-makers charged with that responsibility.

The detailed analysis that must be performed and which will become the foundation of the strategic plan now has an outline. Using the matrix, planners can examine the identified factors to determine their impact, and goals and objectives will begin to take form.

The product   The results of the environmental scan may be presented in various formats. Generally the printed document includes a narrative description of the environment followed by conclusions as to how significant factors may affect the local government in the future. The scan may be presented in summary format with detailed analysis of each point.

The accompanying sidebar shows how the plan for Berkley, Michigan, summarizes the effects of shifting employment location in and around the community. Based on this analysis, the planners can identify the opportunities and threats posed by the shifts. Their next step

---

Environmental scan and summary: Distribution of private sector employment 1979–1988

As a suburban bedroom community, Berkley is very much affected by employment trends in Oakland County. During the past ten years, significant changes have been taking place in employment characteristics in Oakland County which will have important effects on the future viability of Berkley.

In 1979, 23.2 percent of Oakland County's population was engaged in service industries. Service industries include such activities as law, medicine, accounting, data processing, computer programming, telecommunications, public relations, management, advertising, and financial services.

In 1988, the percentage of employed persons in Oakland engaged in services increased to 32.2 percent. During the same period of time, the number of persons employed in transportation equipment and other manufacturing has decreased in Oakland County. Transportation equipment employment decreased from 12.8 percent in 1979 to 9.0 percent in 1988. Other manufacturing employment decreased from 15.8 percent in 1979 to 12.7 percent in 1988.

These Oakland County employment trends reflect larger trends in employment which are occurring in the State of Michigan as a whole. However, the service industry employment sector in Oakland County grew more rapidly than it did in the State of Michigan as a whole. Projection of future employment trends indicates that the role of service industries will become increasingly important to the economy of Oakland County in future years. Future growth in the service industries employment component could have the following effects on the city of Berkley.

1. More people will work closer to home in professional offices, research parks, and institutional facilities located nearer to Berkley.
2. The city's white-collar population will increase and its blue-collar population will decrease.
3. Income levels will rise.
4. As people with high education and income levels come to reside in Berkley, their expectations for public services and facilities will be higher.

Source: Strategic plan, Berkley, Michigan.

Problems	Related opportunities
1. Increasing costs of services	1. Untapped resources
a. Costs associated with population growth	a. Possible sources of funds
i) The youth population	i) Trends toward citizen activism and state spending can help offset costs
ii) The elderly population	ii) A statewide issue; seek state support
iii) The refugee population	iii) A statewide issue; seek statewide support
b. Costs associated with new programs	b. Possible solutions
i) Safety and health programs (OSHA-related)	i) Trends toward federal "hands-off" policy may result in an easing of regulations, costs
ii) Equal employment opportunity programs for police and engineers	ii) Refugee influx may help fill the needs
iii) Programs to combat homelessness	iii) Trends toward citizen activism; volunteers can fill in
iv) Programs to address increase in minor crimes	iv) Trends toward citizen activism; volunteers can fill in
c. Management costs	c. Possible sources of relief
i) Computerization	i) Associated long-term savings will offset short-term costs
ii) Management training	ii) Long-term benefits will offset short-term costs

Figure 2.4. Problems and related opportunities identified in an environmental scan.

will be to develop goals, objectives, and strategies to take maximum advantage of the opportunities and to minimize the threats.

Additional examples of environmental formats appear in Appendixes 3, 4, 5, and 6. Appendix 3 is a detailed summary of conclusions drawn from an environmental scan conducted in Clifton, New Jersey. Appendix 4 shows lists prepared by Santa Clarita, California, of "What We Do Well" and "What We Need to Spend More Time On." Appendix 5, from Whitley County, Indiana, shows a format that allows a quick review of the conclusions and identifies the strengths and weaknesses for local planners, managers, and citizens. Finally, Appendix 6 presents a summary of the environmental scan conclusions reached by the strategic planners in Wichita, Kansas, for the topical area of infrastructure management.

Problems	Related opportunities

2. Decreasing revenues
  a. State education grants declining
 	
  b. Federal grants declining
 	
  c. High level of bonded indebtedness
	2. Possible solutions
	  a. Increasing population paying taxes will help offset loss of grant funds
	  b. Increasing population paying taxes will help offset loss of grant funds
	  c. Lower and stable interest rates; refinance debt services

3. Political issues
  a. Western county residents are no-growthers
 	
  b. County growth exacerbates the urban/rural imbalances
 	
  c. Community/university relations are weak
 	
  d. Uncertainty of a new governing body in nine months
	3. Possible sources of relief
	  a. Eastern county growth means more taxes to support needed public services
	  b. If approved, developer impact fees could provide funds for needed infrastructure for all parts of the county
	  c. High tech firms' growth will be synergistic to the university's evolution
	  d. Unknown

Figure 2.4. Continued

The lessons extracted from environmental scanning form the basis for decisions about goals and objectives. The process demonstrates the usefulness of organizing information in a structured way. One such structure is demonstrated in Figure 2.4, using a fictitious analyses.

Thus structured and abbreviated, the lessons culled from the environmental scan can more easily be translated into goals and objectives. These will be actions through which the locality will endeavor to maximize its strengths and take advantage of its opportunities, while minimizing threats and overcoming its weaknesses.

1.   Kami, *Kami Strategic Assumptions,* p. 2.
2.   Thomas J. Peters and Robert H. Waterman, Jr., *In Search of Excellence* (New York: Harper and Row, Publishers, 1982), p. 285.
3.   *Ibid.*
4.   Benjamin B. Tregoe and Peter M. Tobia, "An Action-Oriented Approach to Strategy," *Journal of Business Strategy* 11, no. 1 (January/February 1990): 16.

Chapter 3

The Strategic Plan: Programs

Once a community has collectively examined the factors that may affect its future, it needs to decide where it wants to be in the years ahead and determine how to get there. Thus, the next steps in strategic planning are setting goals and objectives, devising strategies, and creating implementation plans. At this point, the time frame for planning begins to shorten. While the environmental scan may look ahead for a period of years, it is best to set a time of one year for the steps outlined in this chapter.

Goals

Goals are generalized statements of where an organization wants to be at some future time. For purposes of this chapter, the goals will be generalized statements of where the locality wishes to be in twelve months. Goals tend to be relatively few in number, concise yet not specific, and nonquantitative. The goals in one jurisdiction's plan were simply stated as:

1. A healthy local economy
2. Vitality of public life
3. Quality bricks and mortar
4. Enrichment of the private life.

Further delineation provides the sum and substance of these goals.

An organization's goals may change from time to time, but it is not unusual for change to occur slowly and in small increments. Goals should be attainable yet sufficiently ambitious to make an organization and its people stretch. If a goal is too ambitious, there will be frustration; if it is too lenient, there will be a situation in which less than maximal performance is tolerated. Establishing a few goals is a more productive exercise than developing many. Often, it is useful to incorporate some goals that are readily achievable, thereby ensuring at least partial success. Goals will often become evident after the environmental scan is completed and the resulting lessons are properly structured.

Goals are usually general in nature. Some examples are listed in Figure 3.1, together with the relevant cells on the environmental scanning matrix.

Although these goals are few in number, each represents an ambitious target for one year. And each represents a series of programs and activities. Finally, each represents problems and opportunities. Each will require applying the strengths of the jurisdiction and improving its weaknesses.

Goals are conceptualized and presented in local strategic plans in various ways. The Whitley County, Indiana, plan listed goals in the following way:

1. Revitalize the south Whitley central business district while providing a mechanism to keep activity in the downtown area.
2. Fill the South Whitley Industrial Park with companies that will expand and solidify the community's economic base.
3. A new emphasis on people, pride, livability, and preservation of the past, looking forward to a livable future. This concept will include all aspects of recreation, quality of life, environmental issues, cultural activities, education, health care, etc.

The city of Santa Clarita listed its goals in a slightly different way:

1. Generate a greater revenue base for the city.
2. Stop the movement to have landfills and prisons located in the Santa Clarita Valley.
3. Establish a desirable rate of growth.
4. Complete the roads needed by the community.
5. Eliminate traffic circulation problems.
6. Get City Hall development and construction underway.
7. Provide sufficient revenues to address these major issues. This requires that the community increase sales tax and other revenues.

A third style was employed by planners in the city of Placentia, California. Appendix 7 demonstrates a comprehensive set of mid-1980s goals for that city's long-term future.

At the end of the year, officials will be able to determine the community's success in a general way by judging whether these goals have been achieved.

Objectives

Objectives are the specific, measurable targets set for each goal. They are short-term in nature and there are, typically, several for each goal. Objectives are measurable and constitute the means by which a plan's success can be gauged.

Often, a plan's objectives are broken into sub- and sub-sub-objectives, depending on the desired level of detail in the plan. Objectives

Goals	Environmental factors (from scanning matrix)	
I Identify means of increasing revenues without raising taxes on residents	Cell A-1	Internal environment, economic and financial factors
	Cell C-1	Local environment, economic and financial factors
	Cell E-6	State environment, competitive factors
	Cell F-6	National environment, competitive factors
II Reduce overall program expenditures	Cell A-1	Internal environment, economic and financial factors
	Cell A-7	Internal environment, managerial factors
III Increase levels of service to economically disadvantaged residents	Cell C-1	Local environment, economic and financial factors
	Cell C-2	Local environment, demographic factors
	Cell C-5	Local environment, social and cultural factors
IV Reduce tensions with neighboring jurisdiction or manufacturer who is polluting border streams	Cell A-8	Internal environment, physical and environmental factors
	Cell C-8	Local environment, physical and environmental factors
	Cell D-8	Regional environment, physical and environmental factors
	Cell C-4	Local environment, legal and regulatory factors
	Cell D-4	Regional environment, legal and regulatory factors
	Cell B-7	Public administration environment, managerial factors
	Cell D-3	Regional environment, technological factors

Figure 3.1. Goals and relevant factors from the environmental scanning matrix.

must be stated as succinctly as possible and be immediately understandable.

Like the goals, the objectives will draw upon data from numerous cells in the strategic planning matrix. As an example, the first goal in Figure 3.1 is repeated in Figure 3.2 with examples of several objectives and the environmental scanning matrix cells from which data might be taken to structure such objectives. A consistent pattern of numbers and letters to identify goals, objectives, and sub-objectives facilitates later reference.

Of course, it is possible for different individuals to view the same data and arrive at different goals and objectives. Different approaches are not necessarily right or wrong; they simply reflect the diversity of values and approaches among communities.

Strategies

Strategies are the step-by-step means by which an organization reaches its objectives. They typically constitute programs, events, operations, and projects for the organization to accomplish its objectives. In short, they are the action steps.

Typically, each objective under each goal will have a series of such strategies. These strategies may range from complex projects to one-

Goal I Identify means of increasing revenues without raising taxes on residents (environmental scanning matrix cells A-1, C-1, E-6, F-6)

Objective Ia Apply for state grants in the following three areas: special education, highway maintenance, computerization of public safety response system (environmental scanning matrix cells E-1, E-6, C-2, C-5, A-8, C-8, A-3, B-3, A-7)

Objective Ib Apply for federal funding in two areas: highway construction and free lunch programs for three public schools (A-1, B-1, F-1, C-2, C-5, F-6, F-8)

Objective Ic Increase private contributions to the foundation supporting the public school system by 10% (A-1, B-1, C-1, C-3, C-5, C-7)

Objective Id Increase corporate tax revenues by 4% (C-1, A-4, D-6)

Objective Ie Project increases in residential tax revenues to be derived from increase in home assessments and in-migration by December 31 (C-1, C-2)

Figure 3.2. Objectives supporting a strategic planning goal, with references to cells in the environmental scanning matrix.

time, easily performed tasks. The goals and objectives indicate *where* the organization wants to go and *what* it expects to accomplish, and the strategies tell how.

Goals and strategies can touch any functional area in a local government. Peter Drucker suggests eight areas in which objectives and strategies may be set: marketing, innovation, human organization, financial resources, physical resources, productivity, social responsibilities, and profit.[1] This is a particularly instructive list for local government. Frequently, strategies will be described in detail and will be defined in sub-strategies and even sub-sub-strategies. Obviously, such detail becomes more important as the tasks to be performed become more complex.

The strategies or action steps for two of the objectives for Goal I in Figure 3.2 are spelled out in Figure 3.3. These strategies constitute programs and projects consistent with, and responsive to, the lessons extracted from the environmental scan. It is at this point in any plan that planners and managers can get so excited about new

Goal I   Identify means of increasing revenues without raising taxes on residents (environmental scanning matrix cells A-1, C-1, E-6, F-6)

Objective 1a   Apply for state grants in the following three areas: special education, highway maintenance, computerization of public safety response system (environmental scanning matrix cells E-1, E-6, C-2, C-5, A-8, C-8, A-3, B-3, A-7)

Strategies or action steps

1. Identify grants through published announcements
2. Hire a proposal writer and have each affected department identify an internal proposal contact person
3. Assess which proposals have been successful and unsuccessful in the past and why
4. Establish proposal teams to prepare responses to requests for proposals (RFPs)
5. Establish teams to prepare unsolicited proposals for state discretionary funds
6. Seek interjurisdictional support for regional proposals
7. Establish relationships with state proposal reviewers and arrange visits to permit state officials to see local needs firsthand
8. Publicize programs and facilities that are provided with state resources without raising local taxes
9. Hold openings, ground-breakings, and other ceremonies to highlight these programs and thank state officials
10. Identify future funding programs relevant to local needs

Figure 3.3. Strategies for two objectives.

project development that they overlook or discount environmental factors that can ensure success or impede progress.

Frequently, plans result in the identification of strategies which are important and desirable for the community, but for which sufficient resources are not available. Tabling the concept until resources can be found, or discarding the idea, are feasible options. However, another approach is to identify new resources for projects and programs. If that is the approach that the community elects to pursue, then strategies must be developed in the plan to accomplish the objective of resource identification and acquisition.

Figure 3.3 represents one array of strategies. It is possible that other strategies, even contrary strategies, could also be consistent with the environmental scan and be successful. Strategies are not necessarily either right or wrong but simply one planner's reaction to the environmental factors projected to affect the organization in the future.

Because it is instructive to view actual strategic plans, a strong example of a list of strategies is provided in Appendix 8. These strat-

---

Objective Ib   Apply for federal funding in two areas: highway construction and free lunch programs for three public schools (environmental scanning matrix cells A-1, B-1, F-1, C-2, C-5, F-6, F-8)

Strategies or actions steps

1. Collect data for soliciting funds and prepare materials which demonstrate the need for and benefits of new highway construction for the region, the state, and interstate commerce
2. Prepare materials demonstrating the need for assistance with lunch programs in three public schools
3. Identify, through the *Congressional Record* and other sources, funds for which the locality can apply for these programs
4. Identify federal resources available for unsolicited proposals
5. Examine federally funded programs to assess what has been funded in other localities, and why
6. Assemble proposal teams and submit proposals
7. Seek interjurisdictional and interstate support for proposals where appropriate and beneficial
8. Create opportunities to present concepts to federal officials in person, preferably in the locality where they can view the needs firsthand
9. Publicize receipt of federal funds that allow programs to begin without raising local taxes
10. Hold openings or other events to highlight these programs and to thank federal officials
11. Assess reasons for unsuccessful bids and identify future funding programs relevant to local needs

Figure 3.3. Continued

egies were developed by the city of Wichita for one of several areas for which such a comprehensive list of strategies was created.

These examples of goals, objectives, and strategies may seem ambitious. It is important to state in the plan what can be accomplished in the first twelve-month cycle. For example, creating the proposal teams, preparing the necessary materials, and identifying funding sources may be sufficient for a plan if it is a start-up effort. Solicitation can be incorporated into subsequent planning cycles. This will vary for individual localities. Local governments that have been soliciting grants for some time will be able to mobilize for new program needs more quickly and may have already established the personal contacts that will help.

It is also important that strategies be supported by adequate personnel and budgetary resources. If they are not, their inclusion in the plan can do more harm than good, leading to discouragement and internal conflicts.

Politics is classically defined as the allocation of scarce resources among competing demands, suggested a "zero sum" scenario in which a gain by one program represents the lack of a gain or loss by another. These competing demands should be negotiated during the planning process. Resource limitations should be identified and decision points laid out for elected officials and others who must make the difficult decisions to proceed in some directions and not in others. For each choice, the relative costs and benefits should be identified.

These decisions are best communicated to the affected and interested parties when they have been made with the most complete understanding of circumstances and consequences and arrived at and publicized early. When these difficult decisions have been made and announced, the plan can be finalized, and those responsible for implementing the resulting programs can begin to do so.

It is timely here to mention the special nature of cooperation and competition in the public sector. Businesses compete with one another for finite markets or to develop goods or services which will be sufficiently attractive to create new markets. Cities, towns, and counties also compete in some ways. Cities compete for new corporate relocations because of the employment, taxes, and other benefits they bring to the community. Cities also compete for grants and other financing from federal and state agencies. But the business instinct to protect proprietary information, as expressed in the rhetorical question "Does Macy's tell Gimbel's?" may not be the response of local government. For example, a program which has been developed by one city's public school system to mainstream children for whom English is a second language may achieve extraordinary success. There could be a reason to suppress some of the program's details pending receipt of special state discretionary funding. But in general, there is no reason for one city not to share its successes with another. In fact, those who operate such a program are likely to be concerned with the well-being of all for whom English is a second language and will probably be anxious to share their experience and lessons with others.

Many of the needs that a locality will address over time, then, are not unique. Often, there will be substantial information available on models that have been employed elsewhere in the state or the country. The public planner should be aware not only of needs and available resources but also of as many alternative program strategies as possible.

Implementation plans

The implementation plan takes the strategic planning process to the level of individuals. Prior to this, in setting goals, objectives, and strategies, the planning has related to the locality, the local government as a unit, and its needs and programs. The implementation plan assigns specific responsibilities for those programs and strategies. At this point, individuals and groups within the organization are drawn into the plan.

The implementation plan forms the basis for personnel assignments and performance measures. Ultimately, promotions, demotions, dismissals, and other personnel actions can result from individuals' abilities to carry out successfully the assignments of the implementation plan. Thus, it is critical that this section of the plan, perhaps more than any other, receive commitment from all managers, workers, and volunteers throughout the local government.

Figure 3.4 is an example of an implementation plan for the ten strategies supporting the first objective outlined in Figure 3.3. Obviously, the implementation plan for all of the goals, objectives, and strategies in a plan will be lengthy. Equally obvious is the fact that there will be different options available; the figure shows just one possible set of plans. And, of course, the plans will be much more detailed.

Implementation plans in actual municipal documents often list the strategies and then list the corresponding local official or agency with the primary responsibility for that effort. This style is shown in Figure 3.5, which builds on the goals, objectives, and strategies developed earlier in the chapter.

Another format is demonstrated in selected portions from the Whitley County, Indiana, implementation plan, Appendix 9.

After the planning document has been reviewed and approved, and before it is put into operation, the implementation plan serves another purpose. Since it assigns duties and responsibilities to individuals and organizational units, it provides a basis for developing performance standards. By linking organizational and individual performance criteria, evaluations, and rewards to the implementation

Text continues on page 54.

Goal I Identify means of increasing revenues without raising taxes on residents (environmental sanning matrix cells A-1, C-1, E-6, F-6)

Objective Ia Apply for state grants in the following three areas: special education, highway maintenance, computerization of public safety response system

Strategy 1. Identify grants through published announcements

Implementation plan

- The county attorney will identify and scan relevant sources weekly and distribute leads.
- The relevant department heads will receive notices of proposal and funding opportunities.
- The department head will convene a meeting to plan an approach, collect necessary materials, and prepare proposals.

Strategy 2. Hire a proposal writer and have each affected department identify an internal proposal contact person

Implementation plan

- The personnel officer will recruit for and select a proposal writer.
- Department heads will designate proposal contact persons for their departments.
- Department proposal contacts will meet with the proposal writer to identify needs, funding sources, and general approaches.

Strategy 3. Assess which proposals have been successful and unsuccessful in the past and why

Implementation plan

- The departmental proposal contacts will provide the proposal writer with copies of all past proposal files.
- The proposal writer will assess, for various funding sources, what has and has not been successful in past efforts.

Strategy 4. Establish proposal teams to prepare responses to requests for proposals (RFPs)

Strategy 5. Establish teams to prepare unsolicited proposals for state discretionary funds

Implementation plan

- The proposal writer and the relevant departmental contact person will form a team to work on a specific proposal.
- Other team members will be selected depending upon the nature of the proposal.

Figure 3.4. Part of an implementation plan.

- Proposal teams may identify review teams to comment on the proposal before submission.
- Endorsement of the relevant local elected official(s) will be obtained by the proposal writer prior to submitting the document to the funding agency.

Strategy 6. Seek interjurisdictional support for regional proposals

Implementation plan

- When proposals have real or potential interjurisdictional benefits, the county manager will solicit appropriate involvement in the planning, drafting, review, or endorsement phases.

Strategy 7. Establish relationships with state proposal reviewers and arrange visits to permit state officials to see local needs firsthand

Implementation plan

- The proposal writer will identify the funding source and decision-makers to the county manager.
- The county manager will advise local supporters of the programs who already have or can establish relationships with these decision-makers to request their help in explaining the proposal rationale.
- Where feasible, invitations will be extended to key persons at the funding source to visit the locality to assess the need for the program firsthand.

Strategy 8. Publicize programs and facilities that are provided with state resources without raising local taxes

Strategy 9. Hold openings, ground-breakings, and other ceremonies to highlight these programs and thank state officials

Implementation plan

- Upon receipt of notification of funding, the proposal writer will notify the proposal team and the county manager, who will, in turn, notify the elected officials and appropriate program personnel.
- The proposal team will meet with the public information officer to outline a publicity plan to include openings or ground-breakings, special events, and press releases to demonstrate the benefits of the new public services and/or facilities to the community.
- Key persons at the funding source will be invited to attend openings, ground-breakings, and other ceremonies.

Strategy 10. Identify future funding programs relevant to local needs

Implementation plan

- The proposal writer will identify announced or other funding sources and recommend approaches to department heads.

Figure 3.4. Continued

Goal I Identify means of increasing revenues without raising taxes on residents.

Objective Ia Apply for state grants in the following three areas: special education, highway maintenance, and the computerization of public safety response systems.

Strategies for the computerization of public safety response systems:

Strategy number	Strategy	Primary responsibilities	Support
1	Identify grants through published announcements	City Attorney Director of Libraries	Budget Officer Police Chief Fire Chief Public Health Director
2	Hire a proposal writer	Director of Personnel	City Manager Budget Officer
	Have each department identify an internal proposal contact person	Fire Chief Police Chief Public Health Director	
3	Assess which proposals have been successful and unsuccessful in the past and why	Proposal Writer Fire Chief Public Health Director	Budget Officer
4	Establish proposal teams to respond to RFPs	Proposal Writer	Fire Chief Police Chief Public Health Director City Manager Budget Officer
5	Establish teams to prepare unsolicited proposals for discretionary funds	Proposal Writer	Fire Proposal Contact Police Proposal Contact Public Health Proposal Contact Budget Officer Research Director

Figure 3.5. Assignment of responsibilities for strategies.

Strategy number	Strategy	Primary responsibilities	Support
6	Seek interjurisdictional support for regional proposals	City Manager	City Attorney Police Proposal Contact Fire Proposal Contact Public Health Proposal Contact
7	Establish relation-ships with state proposal reviewers	City Manager	Public Information Officer
	Arrange visits to permit state officials to see local needs firsthand	City Manager	Public Information Officer
8	Publicize programs and facilities that are provided with state resources without raising local taxes	Public Information Officer	Proposal Writer Budget Officer
9	Hold openings, ground-breakings, and other ceremonies to highlight these programs and thank state officials	Public Information Officer	Police Chief Fire Chief Public Health Director
10	Identify future funding programs relevant to local needs	Proposal Writer	Police Chief Fire Chief Public Health Director Budget Officer Research Director

Figure 3.5. Continued

plan, the planners can gain a measure of incremental understanding, appreciation, and support for the plan and its goals, objectives, and strategies.

Finally, the goals, objectives, and strategies provide the local government with an outline of programs, services, facilities, and staff to be funded over the period of the plan. Thus, it is a blueprint for the budgeting process. Once approved, plans will dictate the allocation of finite resources. As noted earlier, funding one set of strategies will, more often than not, result in reductions in, or elimination of, funding for others.

Strategic planners must be aware of the available resources and construct the plan accordingly. The plan may also identify programs or service areas that are priorities for increases, should other funds or other resources become available.

Frequently, implementation plans will highlight recommended services and programs in a tiered approach. For example, if ten counselors are recommended for a city drug treatment center in the base plan, a level of fifteen (five additional) may be listed in a second tier. Or a new service, job placement, may be added to level two. This permits the decision-makers to have the benefit of the planner's recommended levels of service within the confines of existing resources and to select the expansion of one strategy over another. If such options are not indicated, the governing body has no choice but to approve the plan as submitted or conduct further study. The best plans for elected officials are those which provide the clearest set of alternatives and the most flexible format for making those difficult decisions from competing options.

Once a local government is prepared to put the plan into action, it must ensure that the plan is monitored, the performance is measured, and the lessons learned are incorporated in this as well as future planning efforts.

1. Peter Drucker, *Management*
    (New York: Harper and Row
    Publishers, 1973), p. 100.

Chapter 4

The Strategic Plan: Review

The implementation plan is a blueprint for action by the local government organization during the coming year. As the year goes by, managers and supervisors need some means of determining how successfully the plan is being carried out and some guidance on what to do if the plan is not proceeding as expected. Controls, feedback mechanisms, and contingency plans are all tools that can help those who are responsible for monitoring and correcting the organization's performance.

Controls

Controls are mechanisms to help managers and decision-makers gauge the performance of an organization in relation to planned or projected outcomes. Often called *performance measures,* they provide a means for determining whether the organization is on track and, if it is not, for identifying and implementing corrective actions.

If a review of performance measures indicates that the organization is achieving its targets, decision-makers may decide to maintain the current level of effort or to increase the targets, thereby making the organization "stretch." If performance is below expectations, it may be that steps must be taken to improve output, or it may be that the plan was unrealistic and requires adjustment.

Attention to control mechanisms in the strategic planning process is required at three distinct times: (1) before the plan is implemented, (2) during the period of operations under the plan, and (3) after the plan cycle has been completed.

Prior to implementation and as a part of the written document, strategic planners must identify benchmarks that indicate progress toward the plan's objectives. They must then ensure that the organization prepares itself to collect mechanically the necessary performance data, to analyze the data, and to ensure that actions are taken to correct any problems or to take advantage of any opportunities suggested by the data.

During the implementation of the plan these mechanisms must be activated. Individuals and departments need to keep and submit records of activities and progress; supervisors need to appraise the performance of employees; analysts need to monitor performance based on this information. This process will enable those responsible to refine operations as they are under way and react to changes in circumstances or new information.

After the period of time covered by the plan, the control mechanisms will provide the basis for final reports of actual performance compared with planned objectives. Such reports are instructive, as they show the achievements and shortcomings of the organization. The lessons learned through these reports should become part of the organization's body of knowledge to be incorporated into future planning efforts.

In most strategic plans, the measurements suggested by the objectives are actions accompanied by either dates or numeric targets. The latter may be expressed as numbers or as percentages:

- submit four proposals by December 31
- complete fifteen files per month
- provide service to 800 clients
- increase revenues by 4%
- decrease complaints by 2%.

The simplest control mechanism may be a calendar or a "tickler" file to ensure that progress is checked in a timely manner. Often, complex control sheets, journal entries, and computerized management information systems are required. If complex systems are to be used, they must be in place at the beginning of the cycle of program operations.

Feedback

Feedback loops are well-known modeling concepts in many disciplines. The feedback loop is used in strategic planning to ensure that the lessons learned in the current strategic planning cycle are built into future cycles. Such lessons may be explanations for successes and failures, or may indicate the level of effectiveness in reading and assembling relevant environmental factors.

Some organizations build the responsibility for feedback directly into the implementation plan. If this is not the case, a brief special section in the planning document is often used to guarantee that one or more individuals are assigned the task of providing input from one year's plan into ensuing cycles. The text for such a section might be something like this:

Soon after the completion of the period for which this plan is operational, the county manager will call a meeting of such individuals as he or she may deem appropriate. The purpose of this and any subsequent meetings will be to determine the lessons learned in the annual planning exercise and in the course of implementing the plan, and to ensure that they become a part of the knowledge base incorporated into future planning and operating efforts. This will include an assessment of both effective and ineffective techniques. It will also include an analysis of performance levels that can reasonably be expected in certain areas under stated conditions. These findings will be shared with the county board and incorporated in the ongoing planning process.

While this simple statement may seem self-evident or unnecessary, it is a good opportunity for a senior executive to endorse the concept of strategic planning and to ensure that there is improvement in the method from one year to the next.

In this context, it is important to document the performance of existing programs. The phrase "documenting program performance" may also be read "justifying program continuation." The decision to continue an existing program is based on three things: demonstrating an ongoing need for the program, illustrating the success of the program in response to the expressed need, and analyzing the value of responding to the need with a given level of resources.

Thus, if a plan incorporates the continuation of specific services or programs, elected officials must not only be shown that the need is real and the resources well spent; they must also be convinced that the proposed array of services is the one most likely to address the need most acceptably and inexpensively. Similarly, if new programs or services are proposed to replace existing ones, the ineffectiveness or inefficiency of the latter must be demonstrated.

One role of the strategic planner, then, must be to ensure that adequate systems measure the effectiveness of programs and services in meeting the needs for which the operation was first established. This requires thorough examination of both the needs and the program objectives. An example might be instructive.

Several years ago, a small midwestern city launched a program to attract new businesses to the area, but several prospective firms identified poor educational levels and illiteracy among residents of the city as a reason for not relocating there. This information came into the strategic planning process through the environmental scan, and planners believed they had identified a need for a literacy training program. To determine the degree of need, they examined the following factors:

- perceptions on the part of potential employers that the city has a poorly educated workforce
- the level of local unemployment
- the level of local employment opportunities
- the level of out-migration by age cohort
- the number of public assistance recipients and associated expenditures
- the average level of education of individuals age 18 and older
- the number of illiterate persons indicated in the most recent census
- the high school drop-out rate.

Based on their analysis, the establishment of a literacy training program, combined with a public information campaign to encourage young people to complete high school, became an objective in the plan and was implemented in stages over the next few years. Some of the factors that were used to determine the need for the program were restated as performance measures and monitored year by year. Now, as the city prepares to revise its plan for the coming year, the success or failure of the literacy program can be assessed on the basis of the following outcomes:

- declines over time in the level of local unemployment
- indications of changing perceptions of potential employers
- declining rates of out-migration, especially among the young
- declining public assistance rolls and expenditures
- increases in levels of education and high school completion.

It is incumbent upon the public sector strategic planner to ensure that reliable data are available to demonstrate the need for programs and services, to allow decision-makers to make informed judgments, to permit administrators to fine-tune programs and services, and to understand whether the ongoing effort is effective in resolving the situation in the best way possible with the least possible expenditure of scarce resources.

Contingency plans

Contingency plans address "what if?" situations:

- What if the state further reduces grant funding?
- What if the locality bids unsuccessfully for state grants?
- What if an economic recession causes a decline in foundation receipts?
- What if an economic recession exacerbates the need for the school lunch program?
- What if slow housing sales result in declining assessments and less tax revenues?

In its contingency planning, an organization identifies events that are not predictable from the environmental scan and are not anticipated in the goals, objectives, and strategies.

Each contingency is accompanied by an implementation plan to be used "in the event." Thus, managers can react quickly rather than beginning to deliberate at the eleventh hour.

In the contingency situations listed above, the community could find itself facing the problem of public school students with insufficient money for school lunches and declining resources to meet the need. Planners must have alternatives of both short- and long-term solutions. In the short-term, these may entail contributions from local grocers or farmers or the reallocation of funds from other programs. Long-range solutions might involve renewed pleas for external assistance or permanent cut-backs in other programs.

In a business contingency plan, the "what if" question might relate to a failure to gain an acceptable return on an investment, or to penetrate a new market. Contingency plans tend to be different for public sector organizations which are not concerned with profit. A local government's contingency plans may, however, address tax or fee revenues, which affect the ability to provide services, or fluctuations in the prime rate, which affect the ability to borrow money or float bonds. Contingency plans for the public sector may also take account of periodic changes in elected leadership.

Contingency plans may need to be implemented for several reasons. It could be that one or more environmental factors were inaccurately assessed in the planning process. Or it could be that an environmental factor changed substantially, requiring a change in part of the plan. Frequently, such occurrences will be identified early through the control system, allowing timely modification to the plan and programs.

In many organizations, contingency plans concentrate on significant environmental forces which are not foreseeable by the planners—those which result from catastrophic occurrences and constitute emergencies. Such plans may deal with massive traffic accidents, hazardous material spills, industrial accidents, health hazards, sewer main breaks, or natural disasters. In such instances, local governments must have supplies stored, response teams trained, and delivery mechanisms available. And once the immediate needs are addressed, predetermined plans must be implemented to provide medium- and long-term solutions.

These examples illustrate the value of contingency planning. It enables governments to react swiftly, maintain public confidence, and correct problems. In short, the contingency plan prepares an organization for disaster rather than permitting the disaster to take control. Such plans can be implemented in reaction to early warnings.

Although contingency plans often address unwanted or negative eventualities, there is much to be derived from planning for positive occurrences as well. For a business, positive "what if's" may relate to an unexpected sales volume, a competitor leaving the field, or the development of a breakthrough product.

For local governments, contingency planning for positive occurrences tends to be done on a program-by-program basis. For example, when a grant proposal is submitted, plans are in place and can be implemented if and when the funds are received. If a new employer has been successfully courted and has announced its decision to locate its facility in the area, the resulting tax revenues can be projected and their distribution planned before they are actually received.

For contingency situations that cannot be anticipated and planned for, some organizations establish standard emergency response or quick response teams which convene immediately in the case of any crisis to chart the best possible reaction on the spot. This, too, is a form of contingency planning. It addresses the question, "What if something happens that we haven't anticipated?" Emergency response teams may be composed of the chief elected officer, the chief financial officer, the chief administrative officer, the public information officer, and others as appropriate to the organization and the situation.

For local governments, there are innumerable possible "what if's" to anticipate. The sheer range of functions—public safety, education, environmental services, health and welfare, public works, transportation, and more—dictates this. Over time, most governmental organizations develop contingency plans, often in great detail. One particularly detailed and instructive contingency plan was included in the "Community Strategic Plan" for the City of Santa Clarita, California. It may be found in Appendix 10. For whatever reason a local government prepares for contingency situations, the mere practice of anticipation can result in better response and resolution of unanticipated problems and opportunities.

Chapter 5

Organizational Considerations

In order for strategic planning to be effective, it must be fully accepted at the senior-most levels and integrated into the local government organization as both a product and a process. Several organizational considerations deserve mention in this regard: the development of strategic thinking, the effectiveness of the organization's decision-making style, the organization's sensitivity to ethics, and the role of human resources functions in implementation of the plan.

Strategic thinking

The creation of a strategic mindset is vital in the strategic planning process. There must evolve a type of strategic thinking that is directed from the very top of the local government organization and that focuses constantly on issues affecting the future of the locality and the ability of its government to be successful.

Strategic thinking in a community generally evolves with the strategic planning process over the years. Organizations whose strategic planning processes are in an early stage of development tend to be oriented to "number crunching." As the planning process evolves, changes occur: the planning increasingly focuses on issues instead of numbers, and the members of the organization increasingly accept and comply with the planning process and the plan itself. Perhaps most important, the role of the senior managers of the organization changes.

Strategic planning literature and research suggest that the primary role of senior executives is strategic thinking. The higher one moves in organizational management, the greater the amount of time that should be devoted to strategic planning, with a predominant orientation toward future issues. At the same time, mid-level and front-line managers should devote a greater share of their time to implementing plans, with some time devoted to strategic thinking.

So important is the "mindset" to ensure that planning is embraced as a concept and facilitated as a process that many strategic planners spell out what is expected in the plan itself. Often, the explanations appear elementary. Typically, these are the basic principles by which we are taught to conduct discussions:

1. Respect the opinions of others, regardless of rank
2. Allow others to speak, regardless of one's own position
3. Encourage those who are reluctant to participate
4. Support each member of the group to encourage teamwork and pursue a common purpose
5. Promote compromise.

Strategic thinking, however important, is not an easy skill to develop or to exercise. The decision-making process is both constant and constantly changing. It may sound fine to suggest that strategic thought and reflection on the future are deserving of a city manager's or any senior manager's time. It is entirely different actually to find the time to practice them.

Further, strategic decisions often require a great deal of courage. Business as usual is easy, and subsequent failures can be attributed to the mere continuation of past practices. But to risk the survival or success of entire programs, the welfare of constituents, and one's reputation on decisions to move in new directions, can require both personal and organizational courage.

Finally, decisions and decision-making styles are necessarily unique to organizations, situations, and the individuals involved. Still, some decision-making styles can be more effective than others in the strategic planning process. This influence on both product and process will be addressed in the next section.

Decision-making styles

There are several categories of decision-making styles. Two items should be considered in relation to strategic planning and decision-making in local governments: first, the direction of the decision-making process (top-down or bottom-up) and second, the advantages and disadvantages of group decision-making.

Top-down versus bottom-up decision-making   Decision-making in an organization can flow from the top down or from the bottom up.

As the name implies, the top-down approach begins with senior management. This may be the senior elected or appointed official, or it may be one or more of the organization's leaders who have been made responsible for planning. Decisions made at this level flow downward through the organization. Thus, the chairman of the board or the county executive (or his or her designee) might set the general tone and then develop an outline with department heads' involvement. Subsequent input from other employees may be sought, subject to the approval of those at the top of the organizational pyramid. This approach tends to prevail in organizations where initial efforts at strategic planning are beginning to replace more intuitive styles of decision-making in which leaders may either consciously or unconsciously have imposed their decisions on the organization.

In the bottom-up approach, information, ideas, and other input rise freely from the lower or middle ranks of an organization to senior leadership for consideration. This method takes advantage of the collective experience of those who actually implement plans and programs. Data and relevant input are sifted and passed along to be incorporated in decisions made by senior managers.

There are, of course, many variations on these themes. Strategic decisions may be developed using a method which combines the best aspects of the bottom-up and top-down approaches, after which the proposals are merged for final review at the senior level.

Another variation—team strategic decision-making—has become popular. It has the advantage of permitting the planning team to represent all levels in the organization in one consistent process.

No one approach is necessarily right or wrong for every organization or for any organization at every point in time. Localities must decide what style works best for them at the current time with the current participants and constraints.

The top-down and bottom-up approaches both have distinct advantages and disadvantages in the strategic planning process. The top-down approach may not take into full account the experiences of those on the "front line." Decisions made by senior executives are either made without that intelligence or must rely on reports, printouts, or other analyses. This explains why many plans that result from a top-down style are dominated by statistical data, sometimes at the expense of analyses of relevant issues.

Another drawback to the top-down approach is the implication to those in the organization who are not involved that they have no input into such decisions and that their collective experience does not merit consideration.

The bottom-up approach seems to be more egalitarian and democratic. Yet it too has drawbacks. Senior management is responsible for difficult decisions; bottom-up styles vest a great deal of power in those who will be the least responsible for the consequences of decisions and who are least likely to have a global view of the organization's future.

The extension of this problem is that, as recommendations rise from the bottom, each branch and each division contributes separately to the plan. Strategic planners must beware not to permit the total projected plan of the organization to be the mere sum of input from its various parts.

It is most advantageous for the strategic planning decision-making process to include both the view from the "top" of where to go and the view from the "bottom" of how best to get there. Recognition of this need has led to a greater reliance on the group style, which incorporates various levels of the organization in the decision-making process. But even this approach has disadvantages as well as advantages.

Group decision-making   The literature abounds with descriptions of how individuals and groups differ in decision-making effectiveness. The consensus seems to be that groups are more likely to incorporate a diversity of backgrounds and perspectives, which provides a full airing of issues. Many heads are, indeed, often better than one, because greater knowledge and information will generate more potential solutions that will receive general support than any one individual's program. Often, the greatest benefit of strategic planning is that it fosters discussion of vital issues that might not otherwise have taken place.

On the other hand, the safety assured from the greater number of participants in the decision-making process can give way to a presumption of invulnerability, a short step from decision-making arrogance and recklessness. Groups involved in the strategic planning process need to be aware of the available data and the group's accumulated knowledge for scanning the environment, as well as the need for continued, conscious scrutiny of the resulting goals, objectives, and strategies.

In the context of strategic planning, group decision-making appears most useful when issues are new or complex and require a broader range of problem-solving approaches, when it is possible to build consensus, and when it is necessary to counter minor opposition through the involvement of more individuals or groups.

The group approach to strategic decision-making may be of less value when the group does not have adequate authority or when its conclusions are regularly vetoed by the chief administrator or others outside the group. Similarly, if individuals in the group do not enjoy their involvement in the strategic planning of the jurisdiction's future, the group approach may be ill-advised.

In addition to the dynamics of group decision-making, the actual mechanics are important as well. Groups can become cumbersome and produce written products more slowly in direct proportion to the number of individuals involved.

Some basic rules of group involvement in the strategic planning process include the following:

1. Ensure that the group is large enough to incorporate a wide range of perspectives but small enough that it does not become unwieldy
2. Ensure that the support of top management for both the group and the process is clear to all who are directly involved
3. Make available to the group the resources and status necessary to carry out the function of strategic planning, including access to data and people
4. Include the city or county manager, the mayor, or some other key official in the planning process and encourage this person to check with the group on a regular basis
5. Encourage the development of new ideas and programs and creative approaches to existing programs.

If the group begins on this basis, it will enjoy the freedom, support, and flexibility to be creative in its planning and resolute in its recommendations.

Finally, the group must be dedicated not only to the premise that strategic planning is a useful tool, but also to the notion that it is a process that will require single-minded devotion. Strategic planning groups often become institutionalized for the purpose of ongoing review and planning for subsequent cycles. Even the task of planning for a single cycle can take a major expenditure of time. Outagamie County, Wisconsin, for example, reported that its task force met seventeen times and held two public hearings in a seven-month period. This is not at all atypical; the time tends to increase in direct proportion to the number of participants and contested issues involved, and to decrease in proportion to the number of times the planning process has been previously employed in the community.

Ethics and strategic planning

Sensitivity to ethics is important in strategic planning. Exceptional opportunities must be reviewed, but their consideration must be tempered by acceptable standards of individual conduct. When appropriate, planners may even incorporate into the final document objectives and strategies that encourage ethical behavior on the part of those implementing the plan.

Public officials must be ever mindful of the ethical implications of either the fact or the appearance of using public funds or resources to benefit themselves or special interests, rather than the public at large. This includes accepting gifts or favors from those with whom professional interaction might occur, giving preference to associates in treatment or in the provision of public services, conducting outside financial dealings, and receiving honoraria or external employment.

Issues of ethical behavior turn not solely on facts; the appearance of propriety plays an equally vital role. Supreme Court Justice Louis Brandeis once wrote, "Honesty by itself is not enough. The appearance of integrity must be concomitant." This is perhaps nowhere more true than in local government administration with its intense public scrutiny.

Ethical considerations can arise at any point in the strategic planning process. Those who regard and analyze the environment need to remain impartial to their own background, constituency, program area, and personal agenda if the environmental scan is to represent the best view of the future. Clearly, it would be unethical to mask a problem or to highlight an issue artificially through the analytical process.

The projection of revenues, costs, and fiscal obligations of a local government must be performed with accuracy and concern for what is best for the community. If such forecasts are inflated or deflated, the results can be either the unnecessary deletion of program opportunities from the goals, objectives, and strategies, or the inclusion of allocations for which resources will not exist.

While a certain amount of uncertainty in those forecasts will always exist, spending questions can be resolved either by taking a very conservative position or by funding programs in priority order. The latter permits the funding of the critical or desirable programs initially, with additional operations or levels of operations receiving funds as actual revenue levels become more clear. What must be avoided is controlling program approval through the restriction or inflation of resource projections.

The key principle that must guide the process is that the environmental scan is a factual exercise. It must provide the most accurate scenarios possible so the decision-makers can render their judgments about general directions, programs, and resource allocations on the basis of the most accurate and comprehensive information.

The appearance of ethical standards of behavior is critical to the ultimate acceptability of the plan. A few general guidelines can help ensure both the ethics and the public perception of ethical behavior throughout the process.

First, if there is a need because of competition for funds to protect the confidentiality of some information, this should be stated up front, with an explanation of what will be protected, why, and how.

Second, it may be useful to review with those involved in the planning process the relevant standards of conduct in state legislation, local ordinance, and the codes of professional organizations such as ICMA. It may even be useful to incorporate such written standards into the inherent beliefs section of the written plan.

A third means of ensuring the perception of ethical procedures is to provide public access to the process. This can be accomplished by including in the committee deliberations or membership persons who are well-respected in the community, persons of different political parties, and persons representing a diversity of backgrounds and beliefs.

The role of human resources management

Strategic planning as a process will take different forms in different local government settings. Variations on the theme may result from factors already noted, including organizational maturity, the stage of evolution of the planning process itself, and the inherent beliefs and personalities of the elected officials and the senior management of the locality. As has been discussed, the flow of the process can also vary from one local government to the next. And, of course, different organizations will involve different individuals in the process.

Often, the local government's human resources manager is not so directly involved in developing the plan as in its later implementation. However, when one considers the potential impact of revisions to established programs and ways of doing things, and of entirely new endeavors, the effects of strategic planning on the organization's human resources become evident. Although senior managers and supervisors share the responsibility for human resources planning and development, much of the work falls on the human resources manager. The value of the human resources manager in the planning process itself becomes clear.

The functions of such managers normally include recruitment and selection; internal personnel movement (promotions, demotions, dismissals, and succession planning); organizational development; training and professional development; wage and benefits issues; job descriptions, performance standards, and performance appraisals; record-keeping; collective bargaining; and safety. Every one of these areas may be affected by the locality's strategic plan. Thus, it is good to include the manager or managers of these functions in the planning process.

As each of these areas is potentially affected by strategic planning, so each of these areas can contribute to the process of encouraging strategic thinking. Here the human resources manager can play several roles. Figure 5.1 illustrates these roles for each phase in the strategic planning process. At the left are the elements in the strategic plan and at the top are the human resources functions. Each cell in the matrix reflects the potential roles for the human resources manager. The code **a** represents data analysis and forecasting; **c,** communications; **d,** decision-making; and **g,** providing guidance. As one might expect, there are some cells for which a logical role either does not exist or is minimal. These areas are represented in the matrix by N/A (not applicable).

Figure 5.1. The strategic planning/human resources matrix

	Recruitment and selection	Internal personnel movement	Organizational development	Training and professional development	Wage and benefits issues	Job descriptions, performance standards and appraisals	Record-keeping	Collective bargaining	Safety issues
Mission statement	c	c d g	c d g	c d g	N/A	c	N/A	N/A	N/A
Beliefs	c	c d	N/A	c d g	N/A	c g	N/A	c	N/A
Environmental scans: internal and external	a d g	a d g	a c g	a g	a g	a c g	a g	a c g	c g
Goals and objectives	a g	a c g	c g	a c g	a	a c g	a	a c	N/A
Strategies and implementation plans	a c d	a c d g	c g	c d g	a g	a c	a	c g	a c g
Contingency planning	N/A	g	a c g	c g	a c d	N/A	a c g	a c g	c
Controls and feedback	a d g	a g	a g	a g	a g	a g	a g	N/A	a g

Role codes: a = Data analysis and forecasting c = Communications
d = Decision-making g = Providing guidance N/A = Not applicable

For example, the mission statement reflects the essential reason for the existence of the organization. One of the greatest services the human resources manager can perform for an organization is to ensure that all employees fully understand the mission and incorporate it into their daily activities. It should be reflected in the organization's structure and be communicated to those who make decisions about promotions and succession into key positions. It should serve as the basis for orienting new staff and developing existing personnel. And because it portrays the very essence of the organization, it should be an integral part of an individual's performance standards and annual appraisals. The human resources manager's role with respect to the mission statement is first and foremost, one of communication, represented by the letter **c** in the figure.

Other roles in relation to the mission statement involve its incorporation into decisions about the growth and structure of the organization. As an organization grows, its structure, reporting relationships, and culture can change. They evolve either within the confines of the existing organization or as the result of a conscious decision. There is a role here for the human resources manager to provide input into decisions affecting structural changes in the organization and the preparation of individuals to fit into new areas in support of such changes.

The underlying beliefs of the government are not always known to all. The human resources manager can examine these and disseminate them. Like the mission statement, these principles should be reflected in decisions about selections, promotions and demotions, and training.

The internal and external environmental scans identify the myriad of factors which affect the ability of the government to achieve its goals and objectives. The internal scan gives the human resources manager the opportunity to identify strengths and weaknesses in existing personnel, to project needs for new or different staff or skills, and to develop programs to upgrade existing personnel.

Perhaps the most critical role will be to analyze staff capabilities and match them against future needs to prepare for, and to help assess the costs of, the new plans.

Whether the new goals and objectives can be accomplished through the retraining or redeployment of existing staff and resources or through the acquisition of new, the impact will be felt in terms of recruitment, internal personnel shifts, training and professional development programs, wage and benefits decisions, and job analyses and performance standards. Even collective bargaining agreements can be affected. The role of the human resources manager here is to analyze the gaps between current capabilities and projected needs, to decide what actions should be taken to prepare for the new directions of the government, and to communicate this information to the appropriate persons.

The strategies and implementation plans extend the process one step further, to the level of individual performance: that is, who will do what? To the extent that an organization's top management feels comfortable in disseminating such information, this can be vital to the success of the plan. It is at this stage that the plan becomes real to most employees. This is what they will do on a day-to-day basis; the goals and objectives illustrate why.

In this critical phase, the human resources manager must ensure that the "what" and the "why" of the plans are communicated in a clear, consistent, and regular manner. It is rarely enough simply to explain what is in the plan for the individual and the organization when the plan is new; it must be continually reinforced to ensure ongoing understanding, cooperation, and support.

For the human resources manager, there will be considerations beyond the communication of intent and the impact of the plan. There will also be a need to analyze the efficiency of new operations and persons involved in them, to determine the need for recruitment of new personnel or redeployment of existing personnel. Similarly, organizational shifts to support new programs may be detrimental to ongoing operations. These impacts—on the local government as a whole and on the individual—must be assessed and communicated, along with appropriate recommendations, to senior management.

Controls and feedback are mechanisms designed to gauge the progress being made toward the plan's objectives, to isolate areas requiring fine-tuning, and to ensure that the lessons of operating in one planning cycle are regularly and formally incorporated into subsequent plans. The human resources manager is in an ideal situation to contribute relevant data to support these efforts. Where this is the case, he or she should assemble and analyze the data and make appropriate follow-up recommendations.

Thus, the role of the human resources manager is vital not only to the implementation of an organization's plan but also to its preparation. Local governments are made up of individuals and, like individuals, each operates in its own distinctive style. In some, the human resources managers may already be involved in strategic planning. In others, this person may not have such a role. To the extent that the human resources manager has a distinct perspective on the organization and its employees, it is critical to reflect that knowledge in the preparation, implementation, and revision of strategic plans. The result will be felt in terms of the stability and productivity of employees; the greater acceptance of, and response to, the plan; the provision and preparation of required personnel; and the assessment and improvement of overall performance.

Chapter 6

The Role of Forecasting

In strategic planning, alternative future scenarios are identified to highlight the problems and opportunities associated with each and to enable decision-makers to select the goals, objectives, and strategies that are most likely to direct the locality toward the desired vision of the future. Forecasting helps decision-makers understand better the various scenarios. Sound forecasts may lend credibility to some alternatives and discredit others.

The process of formal strategic planning has emerged relatively recently, and forecasting is an even more recent addition to the process. However, forecasting has always taken place in professional organizations, although the methods may have been rudimentary or intuitive.

What has emerged in recent years is a conscious effort to incorporate forecasting methods into the strategic planning process and to increase the sophistication and accuracy of forecasting. This has led to a reexamination and wider acceptance of the methods involved.

Once forecasting was accepted as an integral part of the strategic planning process, the methods in use came under scrutiny. Older methods tended to be most accurate when a high degree of constancy existed in the historical data. Trends, cycles, or seasonal adjustments which had recurred over time were expected to be seen again in the future.

Such approaches did not take into account situations in which prior practice or experience could not predict future activity or events. The accompanying sidebar shows how the fast-growing community of Arlington, Texas, outlined three strategic scenarios to provide flexibility instead of a single "best-guess" forecast.

Forecast scenarios

The strategic plan for Arlington, Texas, demonstrates clearly the value of using forecast techniques to regard the future. Despite their proper acknowledgment of the volatility of forecasts in such rapidly changing areas, its planners relied on a study—*The Perryman Report* (Ray Perryman, 1991), developed at Baylor University—for insight into the future.

The Perryman Report enabled city strategic planners to develop optional future scenarios that would provide local decision-makers with some flexibility within given ranges. Typically, this means that the plan will illustrate a likely scenario and two extreme options—one low and one high. The Arlington plan provides such scenarios of its future economy—static, slow recovery, and accelerated growth:

Scenario I: Static economy The national economy remains poor and oil prices return to $15 a barrel or lower. The defense industry experiences a sudden and large loss of employment due to national budget cutting. The national recession continues well into 1992. The Metroplex economy is static or experiences negative growth in the short term, recovering in 1993 or 1994.

Employment
　　Short-term: Stays stable, or decreases slightly with more unemployment and less work force participation.
　　Long-term: Slight growth of close to 1% to 2% per year.

Population
　　Short-term: Stable.
　　Long-term: Slow growth of 1% to 2% per year.

Development
　　Short-term: New residential sales very weak. Construction activity declines. Office market depressed, minimal retail development. Limited industrial development.
　　Long-term: New residential sales gradually pick up but remain at low levels. Construction activity remains stable, but does not grow. Office market improves, but still weak. Retail growth slow to match population increase. Less major retail, more small retail.

Scenario II: Slow economic recovery The national economy pulls out of the recession. Oil prices stabilize around $18 to $23 per barrel. Defense spending gradually decreases over a period of 2 to 4 years but stabilizes after that. The metroplex economy continues to diversify, compensating for job losses in the defense sector. Employment increases at a 2 to 3% annual rate, led by increases in services sector (3-4%).

Employment
　　Short-term: 2-3% growth.
　　Long-term: Moderate increase of 3 to 4% per year.

Population
     Short-term: Slow growth of 1 to 2% per year.
     Long-term: Moderate growth of 2 to 3% per year.

Development
     Short-term: New single family residential sales gradually increase to between 1,200 and 1,500 units per year. New multi-family development begins taking place. Office market continues absorption of excess inventory, retail development limited to prime areas. Industrial development gradually increasing. Employment growth related to new industrial development.
     Long-term: The pace of construction activity gradually picks up. Office market will absorb all space in key areas, which will then experience growth. Retail growth keeps pace with population growth. Some major retail developments and growth in smaller retail development.

Scenario III: Accelerated economic growth   The national economy experiences a robust recovery from the recession, the trade deficit declines, oil prices rise (maybe to $30 a barrel) and offshore Texas exploration increases. Defense sector stabilizes and hi-tech (semiconductor and service areas) experience growth. Texas economy in process of diversification; receives boost from higher oil prices. Metroplex experiences high growth in services (6% per year), durable goods (4% per year), construction (4% per year), trade (5% per year) and finance (5% per year).

Employment
     Short-term: Increase of 2 to 4% per year, unemployment in the 5 to 6% range.
     Long-term: Increases at 4 to 5% per year, unemployment in the 3 to 5% range.

Population
     Short-term: Increase of 2 to 3% per year.
     Long-term: Increase of 3 to 5% per year, with peaks of 6 or 7% per year.

Development
     Short-term: Single family and multi-family developments begin increasing. Office market in prime areas picks up as excess inventory absorbed. Some major industrial development. Some research type development. New retail developments begin increasing.
     Long-term: New residential development will accelerate. Construction activity increases with growth in residential and industrial sectors. Office market will absorb all space and then experience growth in all areas. Access will become a key commodity. Retail will grow rapidly to match population increase (both major and small retail development).
     Examining future growth decisions for Arlington in light of these scenarios provides a better understanding of the rewards and pitfalls of development. Strategies can be adopted in anticipation of possible pitfalls and for rewards. These strategies and appropriate actions can then be periodically reviewed, in light of changing economic conditions.

The nature of forecasting

All methods of forecasting are designed to predict what will happen in the future on the basis of past performance. Some such projections are relatively easy and entail less uncertainty than others. The difference results from the amount or complexity of the data, the distance in time of the future scenario, or the number of variables which must interact to produce the projected result—the forecast.

Every forecasting technique, however, has some common elements. Although each attempts to predict a future situation, none can do so with absolute accuracy. Forecasts, regardless of the behavior of the past data, are depictions of future activity and future data interrelationships. Sophistication of technique and experience aside, the future remains an unknown. The best forecasters can do is to continue to improve the practice and to develop and hone new techniques.

The selection of a forecasting method depends on the amount, accessibility, and reliability of historical data. Obviously, as more reliable data are available to build a historical pattern, the better will be the resulting projections. The selection of a method also depends on the level of detail desired. As the decisions involved require greater levels of detail in the forecast, the choice of techniques to use becomes more complex. There is a paradox in the relationship between the number of data elements involved in the forecast and the complexity of the technique involved. At some point, the sheer volume of data requires that the technique used be simpler. With fewer historical data points and fewer factors involved, the forecaster can often afford to apply more complex techniques.

Categories of forecasting

Two broad categories of forecasting exist: *judgmental methods* and *quantitative methods*. *Judgmental methods* rely on the collective, intuitive wisdom of those involved. Prior to the emergence of strategic planning and forecasting as professional endeavors, personal judgment was often all that was available to decision-makers to decide where their organizations should turn next.

Quantitative methods don't guarantee either the accuracy of the forecast or the sensibility of the plan. But they do provide additional data bearing on the future and increase the chances that the forecast will be realistic.

There are two types of quantitative methods. *Time series methods* assume that consistent, recurrent patterns in the data can be expected to occur again and again. They assume that these trends, cycles, and seasonal variations will not be significantly affected in the future by changes in the environmental conditions that have historically shaped them. *Causal methods,* on the other hand, assume that changes in the environment will have predictable effects on dependent variables in the future. They assume that environmental factors and relationships change over time and that past patterns may not recur.

Precautions in the use of forecasts

The user of forecasts must be constantly aware of many potential pitfalls.

First, the accuracy of any projection into the future necessarily rests on the accuracy of assumptions made about what data to include in that forecast and how much weight to give it. Again, the milieu of any forecast is the future, so one can never be certain.

Second, forecasters have a tendency to limit the acceptance of their own projections. Due to the inherent uncertainty of forecasts and the human desire not to be wrong, projections are often heavily laden with conditions and assumptions. Forecasts that hedge the bets too much lose much of their value.

Third, projected shifts in the current set of events, resource allocations, or lifestyles must be tied closely to financial planning. For example, observe the hypothesized trends and forecasts for five public high schools within a single jurisdiction, as shown in Figure 6.1.

It is quite evident that three trends require attention. High schools A and B are relatively small. Their students tend to come from smaller families with higher incomes. Further, their family income has grown at a rate faster than the average for all of the high schools in the jurisdiction.

High school C is roughly average in population and family size, but somewhat lower than average in median income and income growth.

	High schools					
	A	**B**	**C**	**D**	**E**	**Average**
School size	550	700	940	1,200	1,200	922
Average family size	3.2	3.2	3.7	4.1	4.5	3.74
Family income (median)						
1980	$28,860	$29,000	$22,410	$20,800	$20,250	$24,264
1990	31,240	32,280	24,900	22,450	22,000	26,574
1995 (projected)	34,890	35,760	25,040	23,020	22,980	28,338
2000 (projected)	39,920	40,040	27,290	24,000	23,650	30,980
% Change, 1980-2000	38%	38%	22%	15%	17%	28%

Figure 6.1. Trends and forecasts for five high schools, 1980-2000.

High schools D and E have larger populations and relatively larger average family sizes. Further, the median income levels are both substantially below average and increasing at lower-than-average rates.

Based on this brief analysis, there may be a need for school lunch subsidy programs for the students in high schools D and E. This may portend either allocation implications for the local budget or formal proposals for grants from state or federal sources.

A final note

Studies of forecasting techniques indicate that one method is selected over another on the basis of several factors. These include the ease of application and comprehension, the credibility of the technique in previous applications, the flexibility of the model to changing input, and the associated costs.

Regardless of the model or technique chosen, it is critical to remember that all of the possible selections require human decision. The relative value of the input is determined by humans. The meaning of the output must be determined by humans. Forecasting is an art as much as a science, and as a science it is inexact. While it helps strategic planners understand various future scenarios better, it is not a guarantee. It simply improves the odds.

Chapter 7

Summary and Conclusions

The basis of this book is that the process of strategic planning is largely the same in the public sector as in a private, for-profit business. It requires similar support among the organization's management to be effective; it requires internal communication to support the concept and contents; and it requires a thorough understanding of the past, present, and future environments in which the organization must function in developing goals, objectives, and strategies.

In neither milieu is planning a guarantee of success or the absence of failure. This was acknowledged in the plan of Santa Clarita, California, under the heading "Disclaimers":

- No matter how much planning we undertake we cannot antici- pate all things that will happen.
- We will not begin by seeking solutions to the specific concerns you may have. We will focus initially on broad themes and in identifying a general sense of direction.
- Individually we may not have all the solutions for the City's problems, but collectively we should be able to get a handle on the key issues.
- The basic process we will follow has been proven; however, it was designed for smaller groups who have a great deal of interaction with one another on a continuing basis. We have modified it in advance for this process, but we may have to alter it as we go along.
- At times you may think we are spending too much time on following the process and should get into resolving the specific issue(s). It is important to remember that we need to follow the steps to avoid misdiagnosing the problem, and to avoid treating the symptom instead of the cause.

While the process is the same in the public and private sectors, there are some differences. The stakeholders in the public process are more varied, more numerous, more vocal, and have greater access to the inner workings of the process than stakeholders in a business. The scope of functions is broader in the public sector. Other differences include the ability to generate additional revenues through taxation versus borrowing or new business development, public scrutiny of the budgetary process versus the profit incentive, the manner in which leadership is selected, and more.

In spite of these many, substantial differences, the order of the process remains remarkably similar in the public and private sectors. The benefits of planning—and the disadvantages of not planning— are also similar. The relative size of the community for which the strategic plan is being developed has little or no bearing on the order or structure of the process. The order of the process and of the ultimate product, the written plan, should be similar for all organizations. And, of course, the direct relationship of the plan's goals, objectives, and strategies to the allocation of scarce resources is a constant from one plan to the next, regardless of the size of the community for which it was developed.

Some things will vary from community to community. Larger cities and towns have more people to demand services and more resources to provide them. There may be a greater variety and availability of relevant data for planning in larger, more populated areas.

Central cities tend to have different problems from those of suburban, exurban, or rural cities and towns. Their problems require different solutions and different strategies. However, cities and towns can benefit from the experiences of similar cities and towns in many areas. Strategic planning is one such area.

Resources for strategic planning

A locality need not advance through the strategic planning process as if it were the first community to do so. Assistance is available from a variety of sources. Professional governmental associations can assist local government officials, as can associations dedicated to planning, such as the American Planning Association, the American Management Association, and others. There are many statewide and regional counterparts to these associations which can provide direction, support, and data.

Organizations which represent localities can also provide relevant resource materials. These include the International City/County Management Association, the National Association of Counties, and others. Again, many counterpart state and regional organizations are also good leads.

Frequently, the strategic planning process can be improved by the use of a process facilitator or a consultant who is sufficiently outside the community to envision new approaches without being hampered by preconceived notions. Often, a person exists locally who has a basic understanding of local issues and resources without being steeped in history or process. Or there may be someone with this insight who has retained sufficient distance to remain unbiased as to the future and its potential. One source of such persons could be the local college or university.

It might even be possible for a local government to "borrow" a strategic planner from a nearby or similar community. This would permit the exchange of ideas with someone who has experience with the process in a similar setting.

Finally, one must not overlook the private sector. Local businesses may have a long-term investment in the strategic planning process and, as corporate citizens, may be willing to share their expertise. The private sector is generally adept at problem-solving, financial and asset management, and opportunity identification.

In short, resources abound. Prudent decision-makers will take advantage of them and mold them to fit and facilitate the local process.

Innovation in local government

One of the primary benefits of strategic planning is that it permits and encourages the emergence of innovative approaches and programs. There is a popular misconception that innovation is the domain of for-profit business, that monetary profit is the "bottom line" which provides the incentive to do new things or to do the same things in better, more imaginative ways. Innovation, however, can exist in any environment. The bottom line to which businesses refer is simply one motivator of new ideas.

A public organization also has a bottom line: the revenue side of the budget, which is finite. As taxes decline or the demand for more or better public services increases, the non-business bottom line constricts. Often a local government has decreasing revenues at the same time it must increase its levels of service. Then a need arises for newer or better ways of doing things. This need drives innovative thinking—the introduction of new ideas or methods, or new ways of approaching old problems.

In the public sector, the need for new programs in the schools, new ways to provide training, or new ways to build roads represent opportunities for innovative solutions. In the local government's strategic plan, it is important to encourage innovation in addressing the problems and opportunities identified in the environmental scan. The objectives and strategies are areas in which innovative methods can be developed. Public sector planners and senior officials should ensure that an environment is provided in which innovative ideas are not just permitted, but encouraged and nurtured.

Planning to plan

One must plan to plan. This is true whether the plan is the first or the fifty-first. It is as true in the public sector as in the business world. The stakeholders in the public sector may be more numerous and may have greater access to the process, and scans may need to be broader, but the process is the same for a government as for a business, and the need for the process may be even greater.

Strategic plans in both the public and private sector frequently acknowledge the ongoing nature of the process. Including a formal statement in the plan itself will provide a constant reminder of the need to reconvene, review, and replan. Such statements may be brief reminders that review and replanning will take place. Others may be more specific as to the timing and ongoing responsibilities of the planning committee. A good example, a statement from the plan of Whitley County, Indiana, is provided in Appendix 11.

Strategic planning can spell the difference between success and failure for an organization. It can encourage employees at all levels to stretch to achieve a higher plane of thought and performance. It can result in the optimal allocation of scarce budgetary resources. It can give employees and constituents a greater sense of their stake in the system and a better feeling about its future and their own.

Chapter 8

Strategic Planning: A Step-by-Step Guide

Following is an outline of steps in the process and product of strategic planning.

I. Identify the need for strategic planning
   A. Explain the benefits of the strategic planning process
   B. Explain the strategic planning process
   C. Solicit support for the strategic planning process from
      1. Elected officials
      2. Senior appointed officials
      3. Department heads and key staff
      4. Citizens

II. Announce the decision to use the process and the expected benefits to
   A. Employees
   B. Key appointed members of boards, commissions, etc.
   C. The press, newsletters, etc.
   D. Citizens and other users of public services

III. Determine the structure of the process
   A. Decision-making approach (top-down, bottom-up, or combination)
   B. Review process
   C. Approval process
   D. Schedule

IV. Select the participants
   A. Elected officials
   B. Senior appointed officials

    C. Employees
    D. Public school officials
    E. External representatives
      1. Citizens at-large or citizen groups
      2. Board and commission members
      3. The business community
      4. Interest groups

V. Empanel the group
    A. Convene the first meeting
    B. Announce, appoint, or select a chairman
    C. Issue the charge to the group
    D. Review the schedule
      1. Meetings
      2. Products
      3. First draft
      4. Final draft
      5. Reporting requirements and the review process
      6. The approval process
      7. Timing of the implementation
    E. Announce support and incentives for the planning group
      1. Rewards of success
      2. Support of the local leadership
      3. Guidance available
    F. Develop committee structure, membership, and operating principles

VI. Lay the groundwork
    A. Identify the mission from the local charter, state law, or other source
    B. Develop a mission statement if none exists
    C. Through interviews and other means, identify key local decision-makers and their inherent beliefs

VII. Conduct the environmental scan
    A. Structure the scanning matrix
      1. Identify the environments to be scanned
      2. Identify the environmental factors to be observed in each environment
    B. Using the environmental scanning matrix (Figure 2.2), assign the review process for each cell (each factor within each environment) to a person or persons
    C. Ensure that participants develop a full understanding of each cell
    D. Reconvene the planning group or assemble the intelligence it has gathered

      E. Describe the possible scenarios for the future
      F. Detail the single description which most accurately depicts the future
      G. Ensure that participants discuss the description of the future for concurrence and understanding
      H. Review the scenario of the future and extract from it:
         1. Internal weaknesses
         2. Internal strengths
         3. External opportunities
         4. External threats

VIII. Review the scan and its conclusions
      A. Achieve the maximum consensus on goals
      B. Develop objectives for each goal
      C. Achieve the maximum consensus on objectives
      D. Develop strategies for each objective
      E. Achieve the maximum consensus on strategies
      F. Develop initial implementation plans
      G. Develop as many contingency situations as possible
      H. Develop plans for each contingency situation
      I. Develop control mechanisms and incorporate into the plan

  IX. Prepare a written plan
      A. Assign writers to prepare a draft
      B. Review draft internally
      C. Revise draft as needed
      D. Submit revised draft for external review to elected officials, civic groups, and other stakeholders
      E. Revise draft again as needed

   X. Submit the plan to the governing body for official adoption

  XI. Publicize the plan to
      A. Constituents
      B. Media
      C. Others

  XII. Implement the plan
      A. Implement strategies
      B. Design and institute controls
      C. Monitor and assess ongoing performance
      D. Assess feedback and revise implementation plans as needs

XIII. Prepare for next planning cycle
      A. Ensure that feedback is captured for future planning cycles
      B. Outline and schedule next planning cycle

Inherent Beliefs

We will be recognized as a community that is truly "a City of the 21st Century" and that serves as a model for other local governments to follow.

We will encourage involvement of all citizens to achieve consensus on which direction the community should proceed.

We as a City will have our own sense of identity; however, we must insure that the [City's] five distinct communities do not lose their own.

We will be known as a thriving, self-sufficient community with a sound economic base in place in order to provide the resources necessary for achieving and maintaining a high quality of life.

We maintain that growth which occurs will be planned and deemed as quality in nature.

We will maximize our human potential and draw upon all the available resources in the community, acknowledging that our residents are our most valuable resource.

We will maintain the rural/suburban characteristics of our community and insure that we exercise self-government to insure that the future is designed by us and does not occur haphazardly.

We will ensure that our residents feel safe and secure in their homes as well as out in the community. This necessitates our providing adequate resources for our public safety mission. Also, we must insure that we adequately plan for natural disasters which can occur without notice.

We will continue to value a government that is open and accessible. Once decisions are made and the various positions considered, we support the will of the majority and mitigate the acrimony and adversity which would thwart the City's moving forward.

We will continue to protect our environment. The preservation of our oaks, canyons, hillsides, ridgelines, and riverways is paramount to insure that the quality of life we enjoy will be in place for our children and our children's children. In reaching any decision, we must be concerned about the impact it will have on future generations.

We will plan the community to insure that it is aesthetically pleasing and that amenities are provided and maintained which will create the desired image of the community.

We will strive to ensure that everyone should have an opportunity to have adequate housing, whether it be senior citizens or first time home buyers. It is desirous for our children to be able to obtain employment and purchase homes in Santa Clarita. This requires us to look at diverse types of housing, as long as the quality is maintained.

We will stress that educational programs be maintained and that facilities and class sizes are suitable for learning. It is also important that we have increased opportunities for advanced learning through the attraction of another four-year college/university to the community.

We will provide quality municipal services throughout the community and not be just geographically based in certain areas.

We will remember our heritage and preserve our historic sites to insure that the history of the community is not forgotten.

Environmental Scan and Internal Analysis

Berkley, Michigan

Environmental Scan: Internal and External Influences on the Community

Distribution of Private Sector Employment, 1979-1988

Two-Thirds of Oakland County Employment Force Works in the County

Oakland County Economic Growth Components

Impact of Changes in Workforce Characteristics

■

Population Trends and Projections in Berkley and Nearby Communities

Population Change, 1980-1987

Residents Age 55 and Older

Berkley School District Enrollment Projects

1983 Per Capita Income

■

Land Zoned for Commercial Use

Vacant Property, 1986

Comparative Amount of Single-Family Residential Property in Southeast Oakland County Communities in 1986

Multiple-Family Residential Property in 1986

Commercial and Office Property in 1986

Industrial Property in 1986

■

Impact of the New I-696 Expressway on the City of Berkley

Analysis of State Equalized Valuation (SEV) Data for Berkley and Comparable Oakland County Communities

State Equalized Value of Residential Property in 1987

State Equalized Value of Commercial Property in 1987

■

Percentage of Housing Constructed before 1950

Change in Percentage of Housing Units between 1980 and 1987

New Multiple-Family Residential Construction from 1980 to 1986

Average Housing Cost

Annual HUD Community Development Block Grant Allocation

Comparison of Results of 1981 and 1987 Berkley Community Opinion Survey Results

Internal Analysis

Administrative Organization

Strategic Policy and City Management

Public Safety—Police and Fire Service

Public Works

Parks and Recreation

■

Community Development, Planning, and Research

Library Services

Cable Programming Services

■

City Attorney

City Clerk

Employee Public Relations Program

Information Management

Conclusions from the Evironmental Scan

Clifton, New Jersey

Employment trends:

- The composition of the city's workforce is changing from manufacturing to white-collar, reflecting new jobs in service industries such as insurance, real estate, and finance.
- With the decline in manufacturing jobs, an increasing number of citizens will have to seek employment outside the city in future years.
- There is an increasing number of women in the workforce. This will create a need for full-time childcare for preschool children, and before and after school care for older children.
- The greater availability of public mass transit, and regional park-and-ride locations, will make it easier for citizens to work elsewhere in the future.

Business trends:

- The number of manufacturing jobs will continue to decline in the future. An additional 20 percent decline is expected by the year 2015.
- An increasing number of women in the workforce will place greater demands in the future for full-time childcare, and related domestic services.
- The greater number of women in the workforce will create more two-income families, creating additional family income and purchasing power per household.
- With more working families, additional services will be needed in the future to accommodate this trend, cre-

ating demands to expand services provided in the local community.

- The local development community is increasingly being influenced by regional housing and financing trends.

Housing trends:

- The city has an aging housing stock. By the year 2000, 85 percent of the existing housing stock will be over 40 years old. The need for comprehensive code enforcement will increase in future years.
- Since the city is basically built-out residentially, there will be increased pressure for multiple-family dwelling units in the future, such as apartments, townhouses, and condominiums.
- The availability of affordable housing is decreasing, placing greater demands in the future for assistance to low and moderate income families.
- A high proportion of senior citizens will result in the turnover of the existing housing stock in the future to non-seniors. Smaller affordable residential units will let seniors remain in the city.
- Increased residential development pressures will place greater demands for "high-rise" type development. Stricter zoning standards may be needed in the future to maintain low-density development.

Land use and zoning trends:

- Older industrial zones are being changed to accommodate newer commercial and residential land uses. This trend will continue in the future.
- The city is primarily built-out, creating future residential development pressures to build on smaller sized lots and marginal properties.
- With increased development pressures, and a limited amount of available land, there will be a greater emphasis in the future on acquiring open space and recreational areas for the public.
- As pressure mounts to retrofit older industrial sites to more modern uses, additional creative development standards will be needed in the future.

Population trends:

- Almost all residentially zoned land in the city has been developed. This will place future restrictions on population growth in the future.
- Any significant population changes in the future will come from the expansion of existing household size (i.e., as "empty-nesters" are replaced by younger, growing families).
- While future population changes will be minor, they will reflect a greater number

of younger children, placing greater demands on the public school system.
- The city can expect an increasing number of smaller households created by smaller family units and one person households.

Departmental issues

Administration:
- There will be fewer federal and state grants, leaving cities to solve their own problems and issues with local funding.
- Any new federal funds will be limited to programs that help achieve national goals, such as affordable housing, shelters for the homeless, etc.
- In order to decrease their reliance on the property tax, local governments will be forced to increase user fees and charges to cover their costs.
- The public, as well special interest groups, will continue to demand more services, but be opposed to increased taxation.
- There will be a greater use of new technologies and labor-saving devices to help hold down operating costs.

Assessing:
- The redevelopment of older industrial areas into residential uses will help bring in new employers and improve existing public services.

- A possible increase in mortgage rates will have a dampening impact on the real estate market, creating a possible decline in future real estate values.
- Continuing property tax increases will have a negative impact on fixed-income citizens. Some form of state-wide relief is needed for these taxpayers.
- More state laws are envisioned in the area of local assessment practices, further eroding the home-rule powers of local governments.
- As county, municipal, and school budgets increase in the future, the number of appeals will escalate accordingly.

Community development:
- A greater emphasis will be placed on creating safer neighborhoods through the use of environmental design techniques, as opposed to hiring additional police officers.
- Both the number and funding for federal housing programs are decreasing, placing greater financial burden on cities to maintain these programs.
- The cost of complying with state and federal environmental laws will be passed along to consumers, adding to the already high cost of housing.

- The rezoning of industrial land to residential uses, due to escalating land values, will increasingly require residents to work outside of the city, placing additional burdens on existing roadways.
- As the housing stock continues to age, greater code enforcement demands will be placed on homeowners to maintain their properties.

Finance:

- Regional job market conditions, and increasing unemployment, could have a negative impact on the ability of taxpayers to absorb rising property taxes.
- The impact of state-mandated programs, without state reimbursement, will place a greater financial burden on existing businesses.
- Infrastructure requirements are escalating and, due to limited local funding, may hamper the development of future properties, decreasing ratables.
- The use of high technology items, such as microcomputers, will be required to hold down rising personnel costs.
- In order to save funds, local governments will increasingly pursue joint purchasing arrangements for common products and services.

Fire:

- The number of fire incidents should decline due to new construction technologies, improved building codes, and more fire-safety inspections.
- Due to an aging population, fire personnel will increasingly become involved in ambulance and emergency medical services to better serve the community.
- The importance of hazardous waste planning and management will increase due to the escalating costs of disposing of such materials.
- As older industrial sites are redeveloped into multiple family dwelling units, this higher building density will impact services and the type of equipment used for fire suppression.
- Future budgetary constraints may require the consolidation of neighborhood fire stations and the reallocation of existing fire equipment.

Health:

- State and federal funds for health services continue to decrease, placing a greater financial burden on local governments to perform these services.
- Higher levels of government continue to mandate health-related programs and services without reimbursement,

which will raise municipal taxes.

- An aging population will create greater demands for more specialized health programs for senior citizens and disabled persons.
- Increased interdepartment coordination will be needed to control the health problems created by illegal dumping and spills of hazardous materials.
- Due to limited revenues, it may be necessary to contract out certain health services to the private sector, decreasing our control over these programs.

Legal:

- The state and federal government continue to enact more laws and regulations impacting the affairs of local government.
- Because of the increase in the number of laws impacting cities, a greater amount of litigation can be expected.
- The field of municipal laws is becoming more specialized, which will require more advanced training in new areas of municipal law.
- Due to the complexity of labor agreements, and the greater number of labor-related cases and appeals, the workload in this area will increase.
- As society becomes more litigious in nature, a greater number of lawsuits can be

expected against the city and its public officials.

Public works:

- There will be a greater deterioration of the public infrastructure without adequate grant funds and other revenue sources to perform this work.
- The decrease in state and federal grants for infrastructure development will force cities to bond for these capital projects.
- The increase in refuse collection costs will require the city to explore other collection options, such as less frequent pickups and charging for other services.
- The "off-site" impacts of development will require new developer charges for such items as traffic control, and provisions for more sewer and water capacity.
- An increased workload, without additional staffing, will require the greater use of new technologies and other labor saving equipment.

Recreation:

- The trend towards a shorter work week in the private sector will create more leisure time, placing greater demands on existing parks and recreational facilities.

- The redevelopment of older industrial areas to residential uses will create a greater demand for additional recreational and park services.
- There will be an expansion of independent sports leagues in the city, placing a heavier burden on existing public parks and ballfields.
- The increased use of microcomputers will help the department to better serve the public by facilitating course scheduling and ballfield assignments.
- Greater innovations and creative ideas will be required to maintain services due to limited grant and private sector funding sources.

City-wide issues

Municipal revenues:

- Decreasing revenues from higher levels of government, and citizen opposition to increased taxes, will require the increased use of user fees and charges in the future to help finance services.

Aging population:

- An aging population will require the future expansion of emergency medical and ambulance services. Modern building technologies, and stricter codes, should make time available to expand these services.

Older industrial areas:

- The redevelopment of older industrial areas will increase the population and place greater demands on service in the future. New revenue sources, outside of raising property taxes, should be sought to finance these services.

Health services:

- State and federal funds for health services have been substantially reduced. New revenue sources must be acquired in order to maintain high quality health services to the public in the future.

Hazardous wastes:

- Due to the problem of disposing of hazardous wastes, a greater number of illegal spills and dumping will occur in the future. A comprehensive Hazardous Materials Enforcement Program will be needed to mitigate this situation.

Juvenile services:

- Greater interdepartmental coordination will be needed in the future (e.g., police, fire, health, housing, and recreation) to help combat substance abuse and related juvenile social problems.

Public infrastructure:

- There will be a greater deterioration of the infrastructure in the future without adequate funding sources for needed improvements. New funding sources will be necessary for this purpose.

Parks and playgrounds:

- Parks and playgrounds are aging and will be in need of major renovations and repairs in the future. A master plan will be required to guide park and playground development and renovations.

Source: Roger L. Kemp, Center for Strategic Planning, Clifton, New Jersey, 1988.

Summary of the Environmental Scan

Assessment of what we do well

1. The City Council is accessible to the public.
2. There is a sense of community.
3. People are excited about the new city.
4. There was sensitive planning in terms of the development of Valencia.
5. There are volunteer support efforts in the community.
6. The City staff is capable and is approachable by the public.
7. Relations between non-profit organizations in the City are good.
8. The City treats all areas of the City equally.
9. The contract services, especially for Police and Fire, are good.
10. The geography, or setting, of the community is a positive.
11. We have a safe and reliable water supply.
12. The Santa Clara River is a positive natural resource.
13. Our parks program is very good.
14. A large landowner [has] positive vision.
15. There is a diversity of lifestyles in the community.
16. It is truly a community for all people.
17. Schools and colleges are very good.
18. Our State Representatives are accessible and supportive of our efforts.
19. We still have an opportunity to plan and create a vision of an ideal community, which most cities do not have an opportunity to do.
20. There is open space available that can be preserved.
21. There is a high standard of living in the community.

22. The quality of life is good in Santa Clarita.
23. There has been a lot of public input solicited for the General Plan.
24. Completion of the river/park study is a real plus.
25. There is a population that will support good amenities.
26. Historic preservation is significant in the community.
27. Magic Mountain is a plus.
28. We have a busy library system.
29. Auto Mall generates good sales tax dollars for the community.
30. We have communities with separate identities, but that work together as one city.
31. We have city management with vision.
32. The community strategic plan is a real plus in that it involves people throughout the community.
33. We have an open government that is truly interested in the citizenry and its point of view.
34. The City is willing to fight to preserve the quality of life and will take on the State, City and County of Los Angeles, if need be.
35. Geographic location: We have our own identity, but we are still close to good recreational area, professional sports, and performing arts.
36. Santa Clarita has had a colorful history; we are proud of our past.
37. The community is in a beautiful area.
38. There are ten million square feet of industrial space available for development.
39. We have a good transit service.
40. Santa Clarita has a strong family value system.
41. There is room to expand and allow quality and desired development.
42. There is a real concern for at-risk kids, especially in the schools.
43. We have strong church support from various religious beliefs in the community.
44. Schools and businesses work in a partnership.
45. Good community activist groups, such as PRIDE, SCOPE, etc.
46. The . . . trauma center is a plus for the community.

Again, these are all the positive aspects of the community. However, we must continue to work to enhance and preserve them. Likewise, we need to address those areas we consider our liabilities or weaknesses.

What we need to spend more time on

1. We have a concern about our ability to address our transportation needs, e.g. increased roads, commuter problems.
2. Day laborers are an immediate issue that have not been dealt with adequately.
3. There is a need to identify an additional revenue base

for the community. Regional shopping is virtually non-existent. Even though there are efforts to develop the mall, the area is currently lacking in this regard.

4. The community is in need of more large employment centers, e.g., headquarters for a major corporation. The City is interested in acquiring quality employers.

5. There is voter apathy in the community. Santa Clarita is not alone in this, but this is a local concern and needs to be addressed.

6. There is more single family housing than multi-family. It is recognized there has to be a balance, especially for those who cannot afford housing.

7. There is limited affordable housing for seniors and first time buyers.

8. Traffic mitigation is a concern which must be dealt with.

9. The community does not provide adequate facilities and programs for teens during the evening to keep them within the corporate limits.

10. There are a significant number of homes, but only limited jobs in the Valley. We need a jobs/housing balance.

11. The community has a significant interest in bicycling, jogging, and equestrian activity, but there is a limited trail system.

12. It is important to share the activities of the City with the community. Public information and feedback is a two-way street. There is concern that the City has not advised the community of its many accomplishments.

13. There is ongoing concern regarding development which occurs on the hills and ridgelines.

14. There has been some headway in terms of dealing with the County and City of Los Angeles concerning mutual issues, but consistent influence on the two regarding the City of Santa Clarita's position on adjacent unincorporated areas is needed.

15. The availability of pure water has been a primary concern expressed throughout the strategic planning process.

16. There are diverse points of view within the community, and these will require people to work together to resolve differences. To date, there has not been sufficient problem solving due to uncooperative relations among differing interests. The strategic plan is one forum in which to do so, but others are needed.

17. There is concern that the General Plan needs to include more areas which are of environmental interest (certain canyons).

18. There needs to be a broader base for community input. There is a need to draw comments and thoughts from the silent majority, as well

as from the various special interest groups throughout the community.

19. There is concern that, even though Santa Clarita is a beautiful community, there are areas in the community (pockets of blight) that are beginning to deteriorate and which require special attention.

20. There is a concern that while some areas of the community have adequate programs, facilities, and services in place, other geographical areas do not. There needs to be a better balance of services and resources throughout the community.

21. There is concern about the lack of enforcement of ordinances that are already in place.

22. There is concern regarding continually increasing school enrollment, lack of permanent school facilities, and overcrowded classrooms.

23. There is a need to increase the number of parks in the community.

24. Oak trees are one of the major natural resources in Santa Clarita. An oak tree is even featured on the City Seal. It is important to plant oaks in our parks, recognizing that it will take years before they mature, but that we need to plan for the future now.

25. In some areas where development has occurred on the hillsides, the hillsides have been graded, but have not been landscaped and maintained.

26. There is concern over the lack of adequate green belts and open space areas in the community.

27. We have never required a sufficient amount of setback to accommodate future objectives the community would like to accomplish.

28. There was concern expressed that there is a need for a City Image which each of the component communities can support.

29. There is a need to establish an Open Space District to acquire and maintain open spaces/green belts.

Summary of the Environmental Scan: Strengths and Weaknesses

Whitley County, Indiana

Summary: Key government services factors

Strengths

- Basic organizational structures are intact
- County perceived as taking leadership role
- Recognized need for coordinated planning/implementation programs

Weaknesses

- Individual community competition for business
- Lack of full-time professional human resources to implement programs
- Duplication of services adjacent to incorporate communities

Summary: Economic development factors

Strengths

- One of the fastest growing regions in Indiana
- Viable State efforts to assist local economic development
- Growing number of improved industrial parks
- Low unemployment rates

Weaknesses

- Declining Central Business Districts
- Relatively low wage scales
- Lack of full-time economic development coordination
- Lack of coordination between County and local communities for industrial and commercial attraction and retention programs

Summary: Housing factors

Strengths

- A high owner/renter ratio creating a greater residential stability
- Quality neighborhoods in some urban areas

Weaknesses

- Lack of variety of housing for those who rent
- Lack of a County-wide housing plan
- Nonexistent or insufficiant housing code administration
- Deteriorating units in rural areas
- Low residential market values

Summary:
"Quality-of-life" factors

Strengths

- Availability of lakes for recreation sites
- Modern, efficient school facilities
- Close proximity to higher education

- Ample land available for industrial, commercial, residential land for public facilities expansion
- Relatively clean environment

Weaknesses

- Limited public lake access
- Unimproved/few recreation sites
- Declining school enrollments
- Limited immediate health care in some portions of the County
- Lack of an emergency response system
- Minimal tourist attraction efforts
- Limited formal cultural activities
- Lack of active "community pride" in some communities

Summary of the Environmental Scan: Infrastructure Management

Wichita, Kansas

The cost of building and maintaining streets, water facilities, sewers, communication equipment, park facilities, and City owned buildings is escalating while needed financial resources are declining. How will the City deal with these problems over the next few years and in the future? The following issues will be covered:

- Solid waste collection and disposal
- Infrastructure maintenance, rehabilitation, and replacement
- Water supply for Wichita
- Wastewater treatment and quality standards
- Streets and highways
- Drainage needs
- Infrastructure growth and development
- Park facilities
- City owned buildings

External analysis

- Infrastructure extension and development provides continued growth of the community, expansion of the tax base, and improved quality of life. Initial costs, however, are very high and benefits are taken for granted by many taxpayers.
- Infrastructure maintenance, rehabilitation, and replacement are essential to Wichita's economic base. Technological advances are making these activities less disruptive and more cost-effective, but the costs are still high.
- The public perception that streets, sewers, bridges, and other infrastructure should last "forever" makes rehabilitation and replacement difficult to promote.
- Federal and state regulations have increasing influence on

infrastructure financing, construction, and development.

Internal analysis

- Infrastructure monitoring and maintenance has been based on structural defects and visible signs of deterioration, rather than life expectancies and preventive maintenance.
- Mechanisms to finance infrastructure development and rehabilitation include impact fees, storm drainage utility fees, user fees, special assessments, and sales and gas taxes, in addition to the property tax.

Goals

Placentia, California

Residential goals

- Maintain the present "residential image" of the community
- Encourage a full range of housing types for all segments of the community
- Utilize available open space to create a healthy and attractive living environment
- Investigate the potential for city participation in future housing programs
- Develop all remaining vacant land in accordance with the city's adopted housing goals
- Continue to maintain the same high quality standards for residential development

Commercial and industrial goals

- Encourage increased commercial and industrial development to raise revenue and employment without sacrificing the city's low-density residential image
- Pursue light industrial development without significant adverse environmental impacts
- Seek out a quality hotel with regional convention facilities
- Develop a cultural complex for the arts with facilities for classes, exhibits and performances

Cultural and recreational goals

- Expand the community building to include a large kitchen and banquet facilities to better serve the public
- Pursue joint ventures with the school district for a performing arts center, the remodeling of a high school

auditorium, and upgrading an athletic facility

- Acquire surplus school sites for the athletic fields and playgrounds needed in the future
- Construct an outdoor performance platform at Tri-City Park, the city's largest park

City services and finances goals

- Expand the city's redevelopment area to foster development which expands the property tax base for financing new services
- Assist property owners with development in the Santa Fe Avenue area, the city's older commercial district, to create a healthier climate
- Provide cultural and recreational services to an increasingly aging population
- Aim to make all cultural and recreational facilities self-supporting in the future
- Form an assessment district, or use subscription fees, for paramedic services, and other services that may be added in

the future in response to new technology

Communications and new technology goals

- Explore the possibility of an emergency two-way cable television system to serve the public in the future
- Set up training programs to acquaint citizens with the use of the city's cable television equipment for community-based programming
- Videotape key city events for historical preservation in the city archives
- Form a Communications and Technology Committee in the future to make recommendations to the council in these evolving areas
- Consider after-hours time-sharing of the city's computer facilities
- Establish an annual Communications and Technology Fair to help citizens keep abreast in these areas
- Underground all utility lines, including transmission lines, by the year 2000

Strategies for Public Health and Safety

Wichita, Kansas

Public health

Protection of the public health is one of the least visible services of local government, but a fundamental activity to assure the safety and well-being of citizens. Therefore, the City should:

Short-term strategies

- Enact a City regulation to prohibit smoking in City facilities.
- Implement approved recommendations of the Domestic Violence Task Force.
- Implement approved recommendations of the Child Care Task Force.
- Expand AIDS education programs to target high-risk populations.
- Evaluate fluoridation of the Wichita water supply.
- Establish an environmental compliance program to monitor City-owned property for compliance with environmental laws.
- Support community recycling program and identify opportunities for increasing recycling efforts.
- Examine the role of the Health Department in the provision of primary health care services of the homeless.

Comments: The emphasis in the Domestic Violence Task Force report will be on referring defendants and their families to counseling and mental health programs. The City is developing its AIDS education programs consistent with the recommendation of the community advisory committee on AIDS. In addition to high-risk education programs, staff now works with local businesses in developing AIDS policies.

No public health program has been evaluated more nationwide than fluoridation. Numerous studies have concluded that fluoridation is the cheapest, safest, and most effective method of preventing tooth decay.

The environmental compliance officer could help reduce the City's liability in real estate transactions and revenue bond issues. A state task force has recommended an increased role for health departments in serving the medically indigent.

Fire and rescue services

Recent technological advances in prevention equipment have not stemmed civilian fire fatalities or property losses. Good planning, public awareness, and improved codes and ordinances are equally successful at lessening those losses. Nonetheless, improvements can be made across the board to stem the tide of fatalities and property losses. The City should:

Short-term strategies

- Assess and prioritize future fire station locations.
- Crosstrain and involve firefighters in crash rescue activities as a supplement to airport services.
- Implement a program that will bring new and existing businesses into compliance with EPA codes that pertain to storage tank requirements.

Long-term strategies:

- Study the idea of building a joint training facility which can provide services for local businesses, emergency response units, the County, and City departments.
- Upgrade the Fire Department Insurance Service Organization (ISO) fire rating.
- Implement a residential sprinkler system.
- Study emergency medical service delivery to determine best means of provision.

Comments: As a City grows, additional facilities will need to be added or relocated depending on development patterns. Also, continued growth demands greater specialization of services such as preparation for back-up airport crash and rescue, and the need to bring businesses into underground storage tank compliance.

Law enforcement

Law enforcement is one of the most basic services provided by local government. In addition to protection of life and property, today's police department responsibilities include public education, technology training, and interagency communications. To meet its law enforcement responsibilities, the City should:

Short-term strategies

- Implement police study recommendations to improve police field operations and case investigations.
- Revise the "priority call" ranking system to assure life and property threatening situations are identified and responded to quickly and effectively.

- Incorporate cross-cultural and community relations into the recruit training and officer recertification programs.
- Establish a community relations effort to promote public education and community contact through programs such as Neighborhood Watch, rape seminars, crime prevention presentations, and the school liaison program.
- Implement procedures to improve crime clearance rates (percentage of cases solved).
- Increase traffic enforcement at intersections with high accident rates in order to reduce accidents at those locations.
- Increase interdepartmental cooperation in enforcement of public health, housing, and utility violations.

Long-term strategies

- Evaluate beat alignments and office distributions on the basis of crime and call-load statistics in order to provide optimal response time for all areas of the City.
- Establish a joint Wichita/ Sedgwick County crime laboratory.
- Provide advance technical training in areas such as special weapons and tactics, narcotics investigation, organized crime analysis, forensic investigations, and bomb technology.
Relocate police operations to a separate Public Safety facility.

Comments: To implement the recommendation in the IACP Police management study would require a massive reallocation of financial and human resources. Some of the recommendations, however, can be addressed through reassignment of existing resources. Planning is needed to identify funds for recommendations that exceed current budget restraints.

A crucial factor in the success of any law enforcement agency is a positive relationship with the community. Public education and accessibility are essential components to such a relationship, as well as organizational emphasis on community relations.

A Police facility in west Wichita similar to the one on Kellogg and Edgemoor will improve accessibility to Police services, increase productivity, provide long-term cost savings and enable the Police department to respond to the law enforcement needs of this fast-growing area of the City.

Emergency communications systems

The City is judged on the responsiveness of its emergency services. Response is dependent upon the effectiveness of the communications system. Failures of the system, whether caused by equipment or system inadequacies, can have serious consequences. To assure the most effective emergency services for our citizens, the City should:

Short-term strategies

- Install a new communications system which best matches emergency communication needs.
- Promote efforts in the Kansas Legislature to increase the 911 surcharge which would allow the City to purchase needed system enhancements.

Long-term strategies

- Move the Communications Center to a larger area to accommodate the growth and development of the Emergency Communications Department.
- Install Mobile Data terminals (MDT) in all emergency vehicles.

Comments: Equipment purchased in recent years requires enlarging the communication center. New equipment is needed to keep up with growth in the metropolitan area. Financing new equipment purchases is a major concern.

Selected
Implementation Plans

Whitley County, Indiana

Goal IV	Objective	Policy	Implementation strategy (action)
A new emphasis on people, pride, livability and preservation of the past, looking forward to a livable future. This concept will include all aspects of recreation, quality of life, environmental issues, cultural activities, education, health care, etc.	Undertake a comprehensive examination of the County's present education system	Determine who will conduct the examination of the school systems	Establish a review committee comprised of an administrator from each of the school districts, a County Commissioner, a school board member from each district, selected chief executive officers of local industries and selected informed residents. The review committee will undertake an on-site review of the facilities in each district, review curriculums, teaching practices and administrative techniques.
		Issue a report on the positive and negative aspects of each system	Using school district resources, the review committee will develop and issue a report evaluating existing conditions and recommending remedial or enhancing actions. The report will be presented to the County Commissioners.
	Increase the number of post-high school educational programs available to Whitley County residents.	Start an education awareness campaign in Whitley County	The County EDC will contact colleges and junior colleges in the area to define scope and content of campaign and request assistance from those institutions. Local Chambers of Commerce will be contacted and asked to help coordinate the campaign at the local level. Local residents will be urged to enroll in higher education courses, with off-campus instruction held in convenient locations.

Lead organization	Completion schedule	Estimated cost	Revenue sources
County Commissioners	6-18 months	$5,000/$10,000	School district operating funds, County general fund
Education Review Committee	12 months	$15,000/$25,000	School district operating funds, County general funds
County EDC, local colleges and junior colleges, local Chambers of Commerce	12 months ongoing	$2,000/$5,000 annually	County EDC funds, user fees, local EDC funds

Vision of the Future—
Worst Case Scenario

Santa Clarita, California

Crime: Crime will be rampant in the community. Citizens will be concerned regarding their personal safety in their homes and on the streets.

Traffic: Traffic gridlock will be prevalent throughout the day, not just in the morning and evening rush hours. Automobiles will be virtually stopped at intersections waiting for signals to change three times before crossing, with increased emissions and driver hostility.

Elsmere Canyon Landfill: The City will fail in its efforts to prevent the City of Los Angeles from using Elsmere Canyon as the site for a landfill.

River Poorly Used: Potential use of the natural resources of the river from a recreational and aesthetic point of view will be lost due to undesirable, improper development and/or a lack of planning.

Water Quality and Air Quality Decrease: People will be required to obtain bottled water from markets, and all yards will have to be desert landscape. Air quality will decrease to the point that on many days of the year, we will not be able to see the surrounding foothills.

Prison in the Area: The State, and City and County of Los Angeles prevail in a unified effort to site new prison facilities in the Santa Clarita Valley. The City of Santa Clarita stood alone in trying to keep a prison out of the area, but, unfortunately, the City lost in court. Construction begins later this year. It will house only the most serious felons.

Failure and Loss of Businesses: There has been a decline in business throughout the community to the point that several have closed and relocated to the Lancaster and Palmdale areas.

New businesses are locating in the unincorporated areas north of the community.

Unprepared for Natural Disaster: A major, natural disaster occurs in the City and unfortunately, since planning has not taken place to deal with it, there was mass confusion as to who had what responsibility. As a result, there was panic and a lack of emergency response and resources.

Slow Growth/Economic Stagnation: In an effort to stop growth, "no-growthers" have taken over the political mainstream and all proposed development is hung up in the courts. As a result, those highly desired new businesses, hotels, and convention centers, once interested in the community, are no longer willing to come to invest in a community in which there is such political instability and opposition to all development.

The Mall is in Jeopardy: What started out as a dream has resulted in a nightmare. The major anchors that had committed to the City have withdrawn from the process. The major financier has gone bankrupt, and as a result, the mall may not open. The City is frantically trying to find prospective tenants and is looking for other possible uses for the partially completed mall. Athletic clubs, bowling alleys, indoor tennis courts and warehouses are considering the building where Robinson's was to locate.

Concrete Channeled River: Because of concern and debates over what should take place regarding the river, it was decided that it should be a concrete channel and redevelopment allowed to occur over the closed portions of the river.

Rampant Hillside and Ridgeline Development: Hillside homes have been allowed to be constructed on the ridgelines. When the sun rises in the east, instead of seeing the natural curvature of the hill lines, the community sees the varied rooflines of the single-family homes strung along the ridgelines.

Sacrifice Oaks for More Space: Development interests won out and age old majestic oaks have been cut down throughout the community to allow new construction.

Undocumented Workers: Immigrants have located to Santa Clarita in astonishing numbers. There is significant unemployment, especially among the people of various ethnic backgrounds. Undocumented workers are living in man-made caves dug into the foothills and are coming into town to solicit work and food during the daytime. This has caused friction between residents and undocumented workers which will soon reach the boiling point.

Gang Activity: The "Bloods" have just identified Santa Clarita as their new territory. The "Crips," challenging their right for the territory, have committed several drive-by shootings in Valencia. Graffiti marking territorial space is rampant throughout the community.

More Years of Drought: The water conservation plan now includes fines of $1,000 and imprisonment up to six months in the County jail for violating the policy of watering/irrigating more than 20 minutes per week. There is some good news in that gray water can now be used for purposes of bathing.

Schools Bankrupt:. School capacities have been stretched beyond reality. One year ago, the average class size was increased to 50 students per class. School overcrowding continues to raise the ire the public; however, the schools have had to file notice with the State that they may soon file bankruptcy unless subsidies are provided.

Review and Update Procedures

Whitley County, Indiana

This strategic plan calls for most implementation projects to be established within the next two or three years, with a number of those projects to be ongoing for an indefinite period. The County Strategic Plan Committee and the Strategic Plan Committees of the four incorporated communities have identified the major issues facing their respective jurisdictions and developed broadly defined solutions to those issues.

In most cases, unforeseen events and circumstances will create a need to deviate from, or alter, the implementation strategies outlined in this plan. In some cases, particularly those that rely upon successful state or federal grant or loan applications, the entire program may have to be discarded or set back in time to accommodate meeting all necessary requirements. Because such changes are likely, a continuous monitoring program must be established among each Strategic Plan Committee to ensure that progress is being made or to modify the objectives, policies and implementation activities as conditions warrant.

Consequently, each Committee must establish a review and update procedure that will lead to successful implementation activities. To accomplish this, the following format should be used.

1. The Strategic Plan Committees for the County and each jurisdiction will remain intact as ongoing committees.
2. Each community Strategic Plan Committee will meet at least quarterly to review the progress of each program to date. The designated lead individual or organization for each project will attend the meeting to report on the progress being made, problems incurred, and/or recommended changes or additions to the prescribed implemen-

tation activities. The Committee will adjust the prescribed activities accordingly, using an agreed upon voting procedure.

3. The County Strategic Plan Committee will meet at least semi-annually, following the same procedure as the community Strategic Plan Committees. Local Committee representatives on the County Committee will also inform the County Committee of changes or additions to their local strategic plans. The potential impacts of those changes on the County's plan will be assessed and incorporated if necessary into the plan's implementation program. Changes in the County Strategic Plan will also be made known, through the community's Strategic Plan representative, to the community's Strategic Plan Committee.

4. The Strategic Plan Committees shall annually consider additions or deletions to the Goals and Objectives statements of the Strategic Plan. Changes in the background narrative will also be considered at that time.

Bibliography

The following list includes supplemental readings. Other journals such as the *Journal of Business Strategy* and the *Sloan Management Review* are excellent sources of continuing research.

Andrews, K. *The Concept of Corporate Strategy*. Homewood, Ill.: Irwin, 1980.

Ansoff, I., R. Declerk, and R. Hayes, eds. *From Strategic Planning to Strategic Management*. New York: Wiley, 1976.

Armstrong, J.S. "The Value of Strategic Planning for Strategic Decisions." *Strategic Management Journal* 3, no.2 (1982): 197–211.

Ascher, William. *Forecasting: An Appraisal for Policy-Makers and Planners*. Baltimore: Johns Hopkins University Press, 1978.

Bandrowski, James F. *Creative Planning Starts at the Top*. New York: American Management Association, 1983.

Bettinger, Cass. "Use Corporate Culture to Trigger High Performance." *Journal of Business Strategy* 10, no. 2 (March/April 1989): 38–42.

Bloom, C. "Strategic Planning in the Public Sector." *Journal of Planning Literature* 1, no. 2 (1986): 253–59.

Bryson, John M. "A Perspective on Planning and Crises in the Public Sector." *Strategic Management Journal* 2 (1981): 181–96.

___. *Strategic Planning for Public and Non-Profit Organizations*. San Francisco: Jossey-Bass, 1990.

Bryson, John M., and W.D. Roering. "Applying Private Sector Strategic Planning to the Public Sector." *Journal of the American Planning Association* 53 (1987): 9–22.

Carlzon, Jan. *Moments of Truth*. New York: Ballinger Publishing Company, 1987.

Christenson, K.S. "Coping with Uncertainty in Planning." *Journal of the American Planning Association* 51, no. 1 (1985): 63–73.

Dalziel, M., and S. Schoonover. *Changing Ways: A Practical Tool for Implementing Change Within Organizations.* New York: American Management Association, 1988.

Drucker, Peter F. *Management: Tasks, Responsibilities, Practices.* New York: Harper and Row, Publishers, 1973.

Eadie, Douglas C. "Strategic Issue Management: Building an Organization's Strategic Capability." *Economic Development Commentary* 11, no. 3 (Fall 1987): 18–21. (Washington, D.C.: Council for Urban Economic Development.)

Eadie, Douglas C., and R. Steinbacher. "Strategic Agenda Management: A Marriage of Organizational Development and Strategic Planning." *Public Administration Review* 45 (1985): 424–30.

Ellis, D.J., and P.P. Pekar, Jr. *Planning for Non-Planners.* New York: American Management Association, 1980.

Freeman, R.E. *Strategic Management: A Stakeholder Approach.* Boston: Pitman, 1984.

Hambrick, D.C. "Environmental Scanning and Organizational Strategy." *Strategic Management Journal* 3, no. 2 (1982): 159–74.

Henkoff, Ronald. "How to Plan for 1995." *Fortune,* December 31, 1990, 70.

Hickson, D.J., et al. *Top Decisions: Management in Organizations.* Oxford: Basil Blackwell, 1986.

Kakis, Frederic J. "Applying Strategic Planning." *Business Insurance,* July 6, 1990, 20.

Kami, Michael J. *Kami Strategic Assumptions.* Lighthouse Point, Fla.: Kami, 1988.

—. "Planning in the Age of Discontinuity." *Planning Review,* March 1976.

Kastens, Merritt L. *Long-Range Planning for Your Business.* New York: American Management Association, 1976.

Kaufman, J.L. and H.M. Jacobs. "A Public Policy Perspective on Strategic Planning." *Journal of the American Planning Association* 53, no. 1 (1987): 21–31.

Lab, R. *Competitive Strategic Management.* Englewood Cliffs, N.J.: Prentice-Hall, 1984.

Lenz, R. "Environment, Strategy, Organizational Structure, and Performance." *Strategic Management Journal* 1 (1980): 209–26.

L'Orange, Peter. *Corporate Planning: An Executive Viewpoint.* Englewood Cliffs, N.J.: Prentice-Hall, 1980.

L'Orange, Peter, and R.F. Vancil. *Strategic Planning Systems.* Englewood Cliffs, N.J.: Prentice-Hall, 1977.

Mason, R., and I. Mitroff. *Challenging Strategic Planning Assumptions.* New York: Wiley, 1982.

Nutt, P.C., and R.W. Backoff. "A Strategic Management Process for Public and Third-Sector Organizations." *Journal of the American Planning Association* 53 (1987): 53, 44–57.

Pennings, J., ed. *Strategic Decision-Making in Complex Organizations.* San Francisco: Jossey-Bass, 1985.

Peters, Thomas J., and R.H. Waterman, Jr. *In Search of Excellence: Lessons From America's Best Run Companies.* New York: Harper and Row, 1982.

Plaum, A., and T. Delmont. "External Scanning: A Tool for Planners." *Journal of the American Planning Association* 53, no. 1 (1987): 56–67.

Pressman, J., and Aaron Wildavsky. *Implementation.* Los Angeles: University of California Press, 1973.

Prestridge, Sam. "The Madison County Turnaround: Leaders Plan, Cooperate to Meet Growth with Services in Hand." *Mississippi Business Journal* 12, no. 15 (July 30, 1990): 21.

Rider, R.W. "Making Strategic Planning Work in Local Government." *Long-Range Planning* 16, no. 3 (1983): 73–81.

Ring, P.S., and J.L. Perry. "Strategic Management in Public and Private Organizations." *Academy of Management Review* 10 (1985): 276–86.

Rothschild, William E. *Strategic Alternatives: Selection, Development, and Implementation.* New York: American Management Association, 1979.

Rowe, Alan J., et al. *Strategic Management: A Methodological Approach.* Reading, Mass.: Addison-Wesley, 1989.

Rue, L.W., and P.G. Holland. *Strategic Management: Concepts and Experiences.* New York: McGraw-Hill, 1986.

Sandy, William. "Avoid the Breakdowns Between Planning and Implementation." *Journal of Business Strategy,* September/October 1991, 30–33.

Scott, Peter M., and Walter W. Simpson. "Connecting Overall Corporate Planning to Individual Business Units." *Public Utilities Fortnightly* 123, no. 12 (June 8, 1987): 27.

Sorkin, D.L., N. Ferris, and J. Hudak. *Strategies for Cities and Counties: A Strategic Planning Guide and Workbook.* Washington, D.C.: Public Technology, 1984.

Streib, Gregory, and Theodore Poister. "Strategic Planning in U.S. Cities." *American Review of Public Administration* 20 (March 1990): 29–44.

Taylor, B. "Strategic Planning: Which Style Do You Need?" *Long-Range Planning* 17 (1984): 51–62.

Tregoe, Benjamin B., and Peter M. Tobia. "An Action-Oriented Approach to Strategy." *Journal of Business Strategy* 11, no. 1 (January/February 1990): 16.

Walker, James W. *Human Resources Planning.* New York: McGraw-Hill, 1980.

Wenchler, B., and R. Backoff. "Dynamics of Strategy Formulation in Public Agencies." *Journal of the American Planning Association* 53 (1987): 34–43.

Worthy, Ford. S. "Booming American Cities." *Fortune,* August 17, 1987, 30.

Yanes, W.B. "What in the World is Likely to Affect Your Market?: Environmental Scanning Keeps Companies Abreast of Sociological Changes that Could Influence Their Business." *Investor's Daily,* September 14, 1990, 8.